BIRT for Beginners

Paul Bappoo – BIRT for Beginners

ISBN: 978-1-4457-4886-3

For Laura, my ever loving and supportive wife.

ACKNOWLEDGEMENTS

With special thanks to Ben Best, Michael Williams, Virgil Dodson, Ray Gans, David Abraham, Dana Guthrie, Raynah Mendosa, Carina Birt, Fiona Foley, Rich Guth, all the current and future members of BIRTReporting.com and the BIRT User Group UK and all the other people who helped my along the way creating this work and on my journey into BIRT.

CONTENTS

FOREWORD

Over five years ago, Actuate observed a movement towards richer interfaces for web pages and the disruptive nature of open source. We took advantage of both by proposing the BIRT (Business Intelligence and Reporting Tools) project to the Eclipse Foundation, which we continue to co-lead. With over 6.5 million downloads to date and over half a million BIRT developers worldwide BIRT is now the premier development environment for building web applications with compelling data visualizations, which we call Rich Information Applications.

This book by Paul Bappoo is a direct result of the community spirit that surrounds the BIRT project. We've been interacting with BIRT users via our BIRT-Exchange community sites, related Marketplace and industry events for several years but it is an amazing experience to watch an open source community begin to grow organically and take on a life and character of its own. That's how Paul Bappoo and *the people behind BIRT* met.

Paul's book, *"BIRT for Beginners"* is a quick start guide for installing and evaluating Eclipse BIRT (open source) and Actuate's value-added BIRT product line (commercial). It is going to prove to be a time saver for people who want to hit the ground running with BIRT and wish to experiment with its various options. In addition it provides an independent critique of BIRT and Actuate technologies and resources that any developer can reference when they need questions answered.

Rich Guth

Vice President and General Manager, Open Source Strategy Group, Actuate

San Mateo, California

February, 2010

ABOUT THE AUTHOR

Email: Paul@BIRTReporting.com

Web Site: http://www.BIRTReporting.com

Paul Bappoo has been an international technical software consultant and computer enthusiast for over 30 years and has an interest in BIRT reporting, enterprise application integration, automated software testing, computer based training and enterprise system implementation. Paul would be delighted to hear from you either as a member of BIRTReporting.com, the UK BIRT User Group or just as an email with your comments about this book or stories about your use of BIRT.

COMPANION WEB SITE

http://www.BIRTReporting.com

On this web site you will be able to register free to the receive all the latest reports, tips, tricks, newsletters and reviews that are continually added to the ever growing archive. There is even an audio recording on there containing an interview with Ray Gans, Actuate's Community Manager in the U.S.

Plus for readers of this book there is a private section (look for the "BIRT for Beginners" link) where you will find additional chapters which you can use as companion reading material and forms that you can use to give to your end users which they can complete to request reports and Information Objects from you.

INTRODUCTION

After seeing a demonstration of the commercial Actuate version of BIRT at an IBM Maximo user group meeting, I thought I would take a look at the free open source version of the software to see how easy it was to actually install and use.

Certainly during the demonstration the software and technology looked rather appealing. The interactive "flash" based reporting seemed to suggest that the long promised and tantalising possibility of "easy to create" dashboard style Business Intelligence reports, over which the end user has an unparalleled degree of control may finally be a reality.

Just to set this in context, I have been a software developer and technical consultant for over 30 years, currently working in the field of enterprise application integration. I have implemented systems on practically every continent on Earth for some of the worlds largest companies. It is rare that a new technology spikes my interest and imagination. So when I say that I spent a whole Saturday (much to the chagrin of Mrs B) downloading, installing and attempting to understand what BIRT was all about, you will realise that this is indeed something worthy of note – my Saturdays are very precious to me!

Working for a software vendor, it was a little tricky to get an invitation to the user group meeting because the organisers were understandably sensitive about vendors using the forum for shameless self promotion. Having been granted the opportunity of attending the meeting I thought I would give something back to the community to show that I wasn't just in it to sell software and services, by publishing the findings of my weekend's toil so that other members of the group could benefit.

As I started unwrapping the layers of BIRT and finding that the product had a lot more depth to it than I had originally perceived and that whilst reasonably straightforward for a technically oriented person to get to grips with, I did feel that for the average end user there were a few challenges waiting in the wings. So I decided to publish a quick start guide to help people in their very first steps with BIRT. This was so popular that I very quickly found that I couldn't keep up with all the email requests I was receiving. The only way to make the report public whist still remaining in my marriage was to create a web site that allowed people to download a copy for themselves.

BIRTReporting.com was born.

After only a few weeks of BIRTReporting.com being made public I was contacted by the good folks over at Actuate Corporation, who (all credit to them) had spotted what I was up to and had taken an interest. This was great news because they were very open about their company and were very keen to work with me on my project. So much so that a few short weeks after that they had given me their blessing to start the BIRT User Group UK.

For further information about the user group and to become a member please visit http://www.BIRTReporting.com.

A short while later, Actuate kindly sent me the two fabulous BIRT Books "BIRT A Field Guide to Reporting" and "Integrating and Extending BIRT". These books are very detailed accounts of everything that can be achieved with BIRT. Whilst they are excellent reference material, they are not really designed to get you up and running quickly with the minimum of effort.

What was needed was an easy to read overview of the BIRT toolset with powerful quick start guides to enable ordinary, non-technical folk to be able to evaluate the products easily before making a large commitment of time and energy. As a result I decided to write this book which is the culmination of my work so far with BIRT and is intended as a quick start guide for complete beginners.

I hope you find this book useful. Please feel free to drop me an email to let me know what you think.

All the best with your own adventures with BIRT.

SECTION 1

WHAT IS BIRT AND WHAT HAS ACTUATE GOT TO DO WITH IT?

I had heard of Actuate before as a company that made report writing software and it struck me as odd that a commercial organisation would be releasing open source software that effectively competed with it's own core products, so I set about finding out what was going on.

WHAT IS BIRT?

Initially I had no idea what BIRT was or what Actuate had to do with it, but somewhere along the line the magical words "open source" had been mentioned and I suspect that this may have had something to do with my new found enthusiasm for the product. So a bit of Googling later I discovered that BIRT (Business Intelligence and Reporting Tools) was actually a freely available, open database reporting technology, that consisted of two major components, the Report Designer and the Report Engine (which is a set of Java APIs). These APIs are also packaged up into a sample web viewer called the ExampleWebViewer – which when combined, allow the user to create graphically rich reports that can be deployed from a central web server into a standard internet browser.

This means that pretty much anyone can write reports that contain lists and graphs and allow the user to filter the data by any column that the report author allows. Naturally presuming that the author has a reasonable working knowledge of the database against which they want to report. Furthermore, these reports can be hosted on a central server in an organisations intranet or even on a publically available web server and can be viewed by anyone who has a copy of Internet Explorer handy on their PC (so that's just about everyone then). Of course the other main browsers are supported too.

I have run BIRT on many flavours of virtual machine, from Microsoft's Virtual PC to VM Ware and my favourite, Sun Microsystems' Virtual Box. In my experience it runs just fine on all of them, given a host PC with a dual core processor and 2 GB or RAM, with one of those given over to the virtual environment. I have also run BIRT on Windows XP, Windows Vista, Windows 7 and Ubuntu 9.10, all with great success.

There is even a copy of BIRT pre-installed on Ubuntu, on a virtual machine, which can be purchased from BIRTReporting.com if you would like to get started quickly.

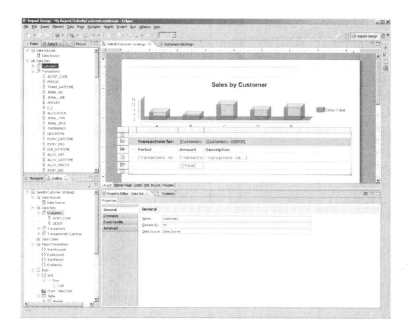

The BIRT Report Designer within Eclipse.

WHAT DO YOU NEED?

At first I discovered that in order to create a BIRT report one required a copy of something called Eclipse. This turned out to be a freely available, open source Integrated Development Environment (IDE) into which one installs the BIRT designer components. When components are installed into Eclipse it is referred to as a perspective – which is why my first publication was called "BIRT – a newbie's perspective" – I'm not sure if anyone got it but I thought it was funny! Anyway I made my first goal to install a copy of Eclipse with these components installed.

Google soon pointed me in the right direction to obtain the relevant software and as you will see later on, it is possible to download a copy of the Eclipse IDE which includes the BIRT perspective, built in, right out of the download, as it were. With this in hand, in no time I was able to follow a tutorial on how to build my first BIRT report.

THE ECLIPSE DESIGNER

At this stage I was beginning to be impressed – the report designer is clearly and logically laid out and basic listing reports are created in a similar manner to creating an HTML table in a WYSIWYG web design package. The downloadable components even include a database against which you can build your first report. This was a godsend because I had no idea how to connect the report designer to one of my existing SQL Server databases. After creating my demo report this was my next challenge.

CONNECTING TO SQL SERVER

Again turning to Google, I found the wonderfully informative BIRT forums, which pointed me in the direction of a great Java component called JTDS. According to the forums this was faster and more reliable than the Microsoft JDBC connector. Once I had this in place I was very easily able to connect to my SQL server and access the tables. Initially I had a small problem with this whereby I was unable to browse the database tables from within the BIRT / Eclipse environment, but as long as I knew the table and field names that I was after, this did not present a significant difficulty. Ultimately I found an answer to the issue with the help of Michael Williams, who is an associate evangelist at Actuate. I posted a question on the forums at BIRT-Exchange.org and in no time Michael had responded.

In case you have the same problem the answer is, within the BIRT Perspective, to go to *Window / Preferences / Report Design / Data Set Editor / JDBC Data Se*t and increase the number of schemas to display and the number of tables within each schema to display.

GETTING AMBITIOUS

Before long I had created a report which combined data from two tables into a third, from which the ultimate report would run. I even ventured as far as creating four separate report variables, which would allow the user to enter parameters such as a period and account range, against which the report would filter. Having gained some confidence by this stage, I was able to apply a bar chart above my data table and even an image to the header of the report. Every step of the way I could preview my report in the report viewer. Very soon after I came up with a result that I was reasonably happy with.

Having written a parameter driven report, containing advanced components and a complex data source, my next challenge was to publish it to a browser.

PUBLISHING TO A BROWSER

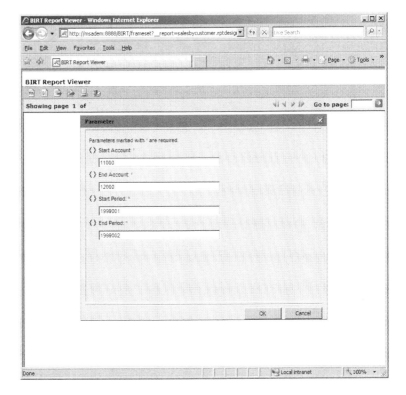

The parameter entry screen of my report running in Internet Explorer

For this I discovered that I needed a copy of the Tomcat web server, again freely available online. I downloaded and installed Tomcat, put my report in the folder, where I was supposed to put it according to the instructions and found out – it didn't work! In order to solve the problem I had to copy my JTDS driver into the Tomcat server framework and restart the Tomcat service. Then I was able to point a web browser from another machine across the network at my Web server to run my report from all the way across my living room!

WHAT DOES ACTUATE ADD?

One of the exciting things about the demonstration that we saw on the user group day was the ability for the report user to physically tweak a flash control that looked a bit like a VU meter and have the report data modified to reflect the change in real time.

This turns out to be one of the key differences between what you can download and use for free and what you get if you buy the BIRT add-ons from Actuate. Also available as commercial options are something called iServer Express and the Actuate BIRT Report Studio, which when used together can allow end users the ability to write their own reports in their web browser and save them to a central, manageable repository. All pretty cool stuff, which I look at in detail throughout the pages of this book.

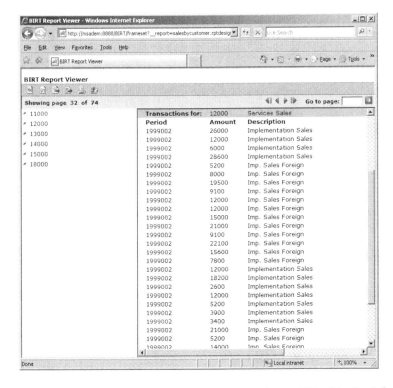

A simple BIRT report grouped by account code — BIRT adds the left hand content pane automatically. It is active, so clicking on an account displays that section of the report!

IN A NUTSHELL

In conclusion, the freely available BIRT reporting tools running on the Eclipse and Tomcat combination allow intermediate level users to create and deploy graphically rich, parameter driven reports. The report designer does need a good understanding of the source database and these reports are not capable of using the advanced, real time, flash based Actuate tools, but still offer an easy to use reporting environment with a result that is easy to deploy across the enterprise.

SECTION 2

THE COMPLETE GETTING STARTED GUIDE TO BIRT REPORTING

Starting out with BIRT report writing? Learn where to download the components, how to install them, how to get started writing reports against your own database and how to deploy your reports to remote web browsers.

ABOUT BIRT

One of the things I found when I embarked on this project was that there were quite a few components that needed to be downloaded, installed and configured. Not only this but since these components are all open source, there are uncompiled versions available as well as different compiled versions. Because I was simply interested in being able to create reports, I decided to go for pre-compiled versions. Even then I had to spend a bit of time actually finding versions of all the various components that would comfortably work together and allow me to access my own databases.

Obviously software versions may have changed since I wrote this so lookout for new releases of the various components. I have listed the sites where I downloaded the various files but there are many mirrors out there so you may be better off just doing a search for the file names. Do be sure to scan each file for viruses before you unpack it!

I installed the whole kit onto a virtual machine to avoid breaking my main PC and have tried this on the Microsoft Virtual PC, VM Ware and Sun Virtual Box all with great success.

There is a video tutorial available to purchase on the BIRTReporting.com web site which walks you through the following installation steps in real time. This video demonstates that it is possible to have BIRT up and running and be creating reports in just 30 minutes!

DOWNLOADING THE SOFTWARE

ECLIPSE

The BIRT report designer runs within the Eclipse Integrated Development Environment (IDE) so start first by downloading a copy of Eclipse.

I downloaded an *"AllInOne"* package for Windows which is pre-compiled and comes with all the dependencies required to run the BIRT report designer in the Eclipse environment from here:

http://mirrors.ibiblio.org/pub/mirrors/eclipse/technology/epp/dow nloads/release/galileo/R

Look for the *"Eclipse-reporting-galileo-win32.zip"* link.

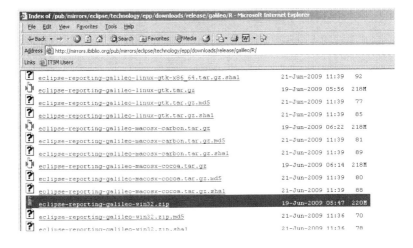

JAVA VIRTUAL MACHINE

You need Java installed to run Eclipse and I downloaded the Java runtime environment from Sun Microsystems at this address:

http://www.java.com/en/download/

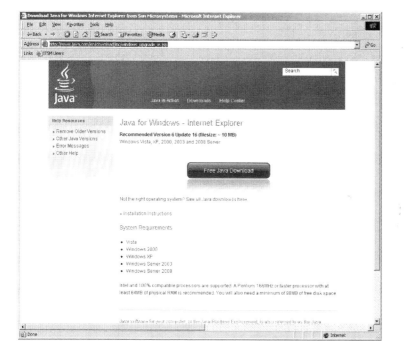

SQL DATABASE DRIVER

To be able to source data from MS SQL server you will need a database connectivity component. After looking around a bit the recommended way of doing this seemed to be to use the JTDS data driver, which I downloaded from here:

http://sourceforge.net/projects/jtds/files/

Look for the *"jtds-1.2.3-dist.zip"* link

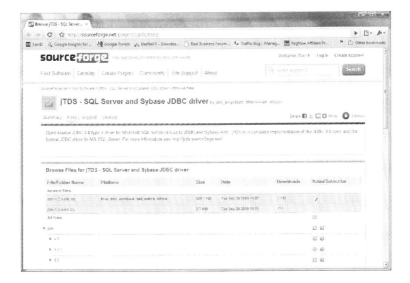

BIRT RUNTIME

To deploy your reports you will need the BIRT runtime which I downloaded from:

http://www.mirrorservice.org/sites/download.eclipse.org/eclipseMirror/birt/downloads/drops/

Look for the *"BIRT-runtime-2_5_0.zip"* link in the latest release directory

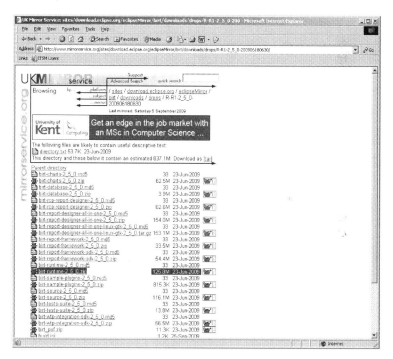

APACHE TOMCAT

You will also need an application server on which to host your reports. Tomcat is ideal and the download is available from:

http://people.apache.org/~remm/tomcat-6/v6.0.20/bin/

Look for the *"apache-tomcat-6.0.20.exe"* link

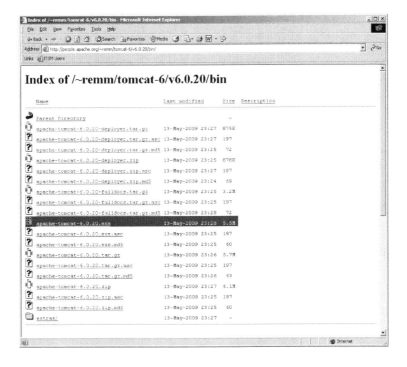

COMMONS LOGGING

Finally you will need the commons logging add-in for Tomcat Which I found here:

http://www.apache.org/dist/commons/logging/binaries/

Look for the *"commons-logging-1.1.1-bin.zip"* link

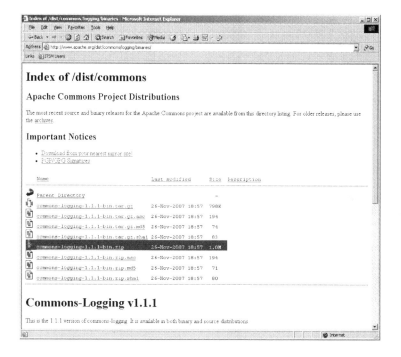

SUMMARY OF FILES REQUIRED

Filename
Eclipse-reporting-galileo-win32.zip
jre-6u16-windows-i586-s.exe
jtds-1.2.3-dist.zip
BIRT-runtime-2_5_0.zip
apache-tomcat-6.0.20.exe
commons-logging-1.1.1-bin.zip

Bear in mind that software versions will change quickly and the locations I downloaded my initial copies from were version specific. To get the latest versions the best locations to try are:

http://www.eclipse.org/birt

http://www.birt-exchange.com/be/downloads

http://www.java.com

http://tomcat.apache.org/

http://commons.apache.org/logging/

http://sourceforge.net/projects/jtds/files/

REPORT WRITER INSTALLATION

If you have any of these components already installed then you can skip the installation, but do check to make sure you have the correct versions. It is possible to have multiple versions of most (if not all) of these files installed, so you may wish to install a second version if your existing version is older but still in use.

For example you can have multiple versions of the Java runtime on a single PC and when you set up your applications you can explicitly tell them which version to use. Some applications, like Eclipse, allow this to be specified on the command line and others need the path environment variable to contain the path to the required component. We look at how this is achieved in the following pages.

JAVA RUNTIME

Launch jre-6u16-windows-i586-s.exe

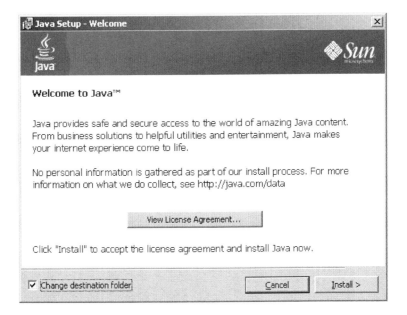

If you want to change the default installation location be sure to check the box in the lower left hand corner, although the default is suitable for most people. Then just follow the installation wizard accepting the defaults.

ECLIPSE

Next unzip the eclipse-reporting-galileo-win32.zip. There is no further installation required – it just runs from where it is unzipped to, so put in into a suitable location. On Windows machines you can place it into the Program Files area to be consistent with the rest of your programs.

Then just launch eclipse.exe from the installation location.

Eclipse is dependent on the Java platform so if you get a message similar to the following, it means that Eclipse can't find the version of Java that you have just installed. This may happen if you have an earlier version of Java on your machine.

To fix this you could simply add the path to the Java virtual machine to your system path, or you can create a shortcut to eclipse.exe which contains an explicit pointer to the correct Java runtime to use. This is the command line I use:

"C:\Program Files\eclipse\eclipse.exe" -vm "C:\Program Files\Java\jre6\bin\client"

If you have spaces in your path e.g. between "Program" and "Files" as I do, then be sure to include the entire path in quotes as I have done in this example.

When you launch Eclipse from your shortcut you should see the workspace selector.

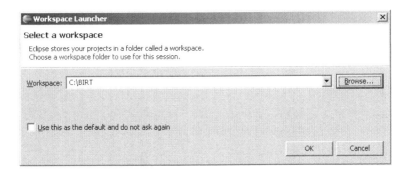

Select a suitable location for Eclipse to store your projects in and tick the "Use this as the default…" checkbox so you don't have to make this selection again.

If you have been successful you will see the Welcome screen.

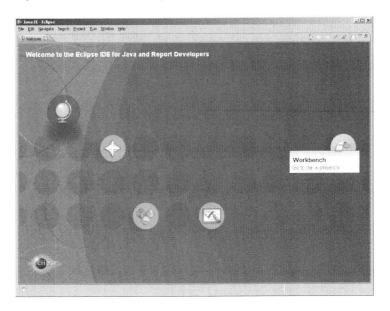

Hover your mouse over the various icons to see what they do, the one on the far right is the Eclipse IDE workbench. Clicking on this opens the main designer window.

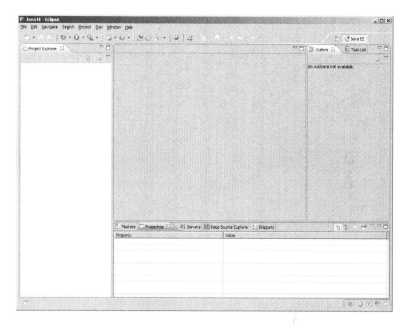

*The Eclipse **IDE***

You are currently not seeing BIRT within Eclipse. BIRT is what is known as a Perspective and to open it go to the Window menu and select:

➤   *OPEN PERSPECTIVE*

➤   *REPORT DESIGN*

If Report Design is not available on the menu, select:

> *OTHER*

> *REPORT DESIGN*

from the list that appears.

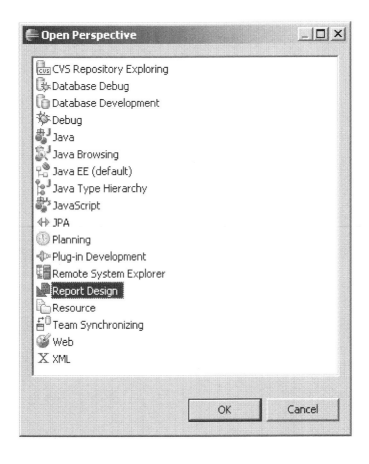

YOUR FIRST BIRT REPORT

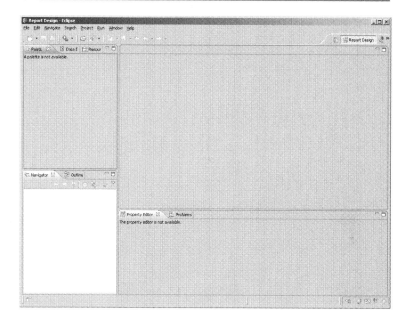

The BIRT perspective is displayed, notice how the panes are re-arranged to the BIRT view of the world.

CREATE THE PROJECT

You are now ready to create your first BIRT report. Select:

- ➤ *FILE*

- ➤ *NEW*

- ➤ *PROJECT*

and in the window that opens select

- ➤ *BUSINESS INTELLIGENCE AND REPORTING TOOLS*

- ➤ *REPORT PROJECT*

and click Next.

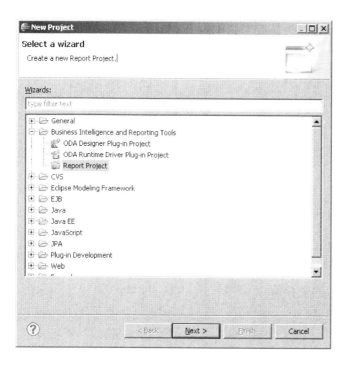

Enter a name for your project, like My First BIRT report and notice that the default path is chosen for you as the one you selected when launching the application earlier.

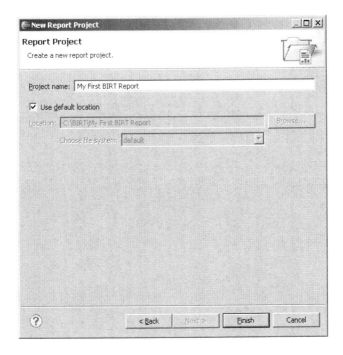

Click Finish. Your project is created in the lower left hand pane.

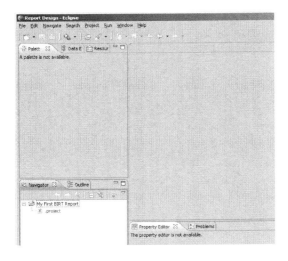

CREATE YOUR REPORT

To create a report within your project select:

- ➤ *FILE*

- ➤ *NEW*

- ➤ *REPORT*

and in the window that is displayed select *"My First BIRT Report"* or whatever you called the project and enter a name for your report in the lower text field, like *MyReport.rptdesign*

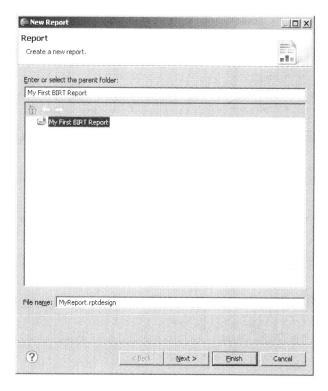

Click Next

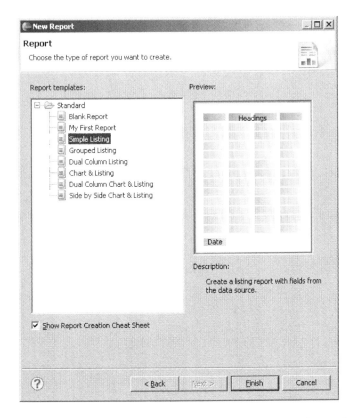

BIRT Provides a number of report style templates to choose from, it's probably a good idea to start with a simple listing report for now.

SELECT SIMPLE LISTING AND CLICK FINISH.

Notice how the Palette, data sources and resources are populated with the various tools you will need to create your report. Also the main central window is populated with the report canvas which already contains a table. This is because you selected the Simple Listing template, if you had selected a blank report then the table would not be created for you.

The property editor is displayed in the lower half of the central window and on the right is the Cheat Sheets area, where you will find a full BIRT tutorial. Make a mental note of how to get back to this for more advanced information at a later stage. For now carry on through this simple guide to creating your first report against your own database.

USING YOUR OWN DATABASE

The demonstration database is a good place to get started but if you want to start reporting on your own data then you will need to install a suitable data access component.

You have already downloaded the JTDS database driver for MS SQL Server. You can of course download other drivers for other databases, but for this guide we will focus on using MS SQL.

INSTALLING THE MS SQL DRIVER

Start by unzipping the *JTDS-1.2.3-dist.zip* into a folder within the Eclipse installation directory. Next, from the BIRT report designer

> ➢ *RIGHT CLICK ON DATA SOURCES*

> ➢ *SELECT NEW DATA SOURCE*

> ➢ *SELECT JDBC DATA SOURCE*

enter a suitable name for your new data source and click *Next*

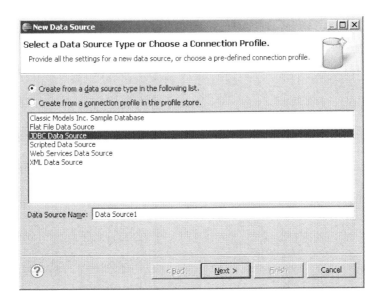

Now click *Manage Drivers*

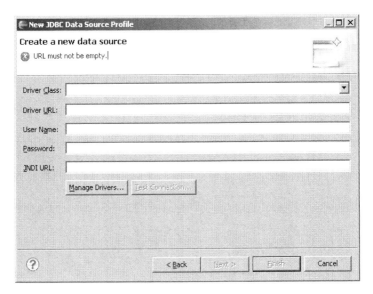

Then click *Add* and navigate to where you unzipped the JTDS package earlier, then select the

JTDS-1.2.3.jar file.

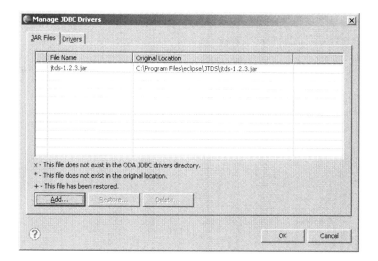

The driver file will be displayed in the JAR Files grid. Click on the *Drivers* tab and ensure that the driver is visible in the list, then click OK.

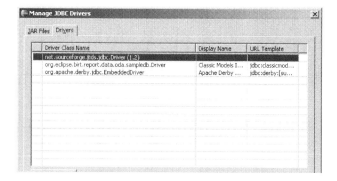

CONNECT TO YOUR DATABASE

Complete the form as in the screenshot to point to your database.

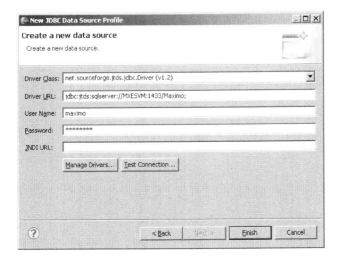

The default port for SQL Server is *1433* and the Driver URL breaks down as follows:

jdbc:jtds:sqlserver://server[:port][/database];

After testing the connection and receiving the connection successful message click Finish.

DATABASE CONNECTION ERRORS

If you experience errors connecting to your database with SQL server and JTDS then here is something to try.

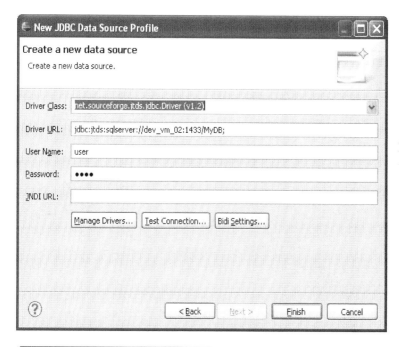

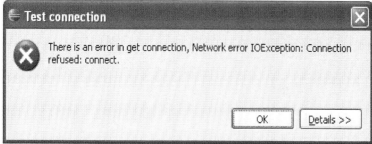

On testing the connection you may see something like this, in which case see if you can connect to the SQL Server using Telnet.

Open a command prompt and type the command

Telnet <servername> 1433

where <servername> is the name or IP Address of the SQL server.

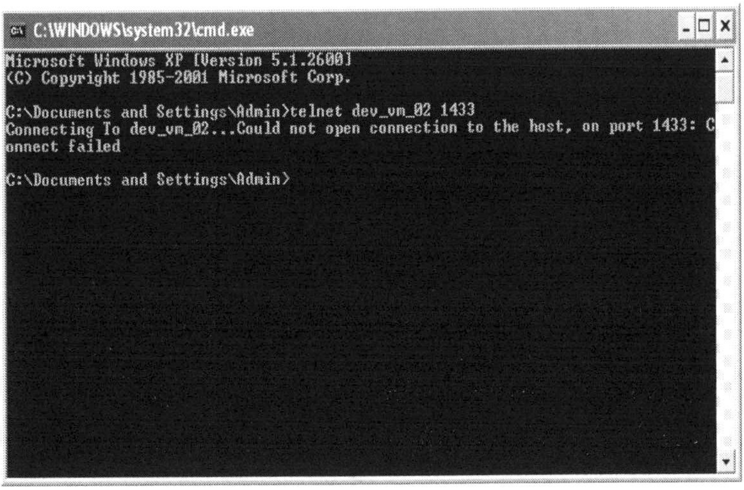

If this returns a connection error as in the screen shot above, then ensure that the port 1433 is not being blocked by a firewall or in use by another application.

If the port is open it is possible that SQL Server may not be allowing remote access.

To check for this launch the SQL Server Surface Area Configuration tool which is usually located in

➢ *Start*

➢ *All Programs*

➢ *Microsoft SQL Server 2005*

➢ *Configuration Tools*

➢ *SQL Server Surface Area Configuration*

This applies to SQL Server 2005 but is similar for 2008.

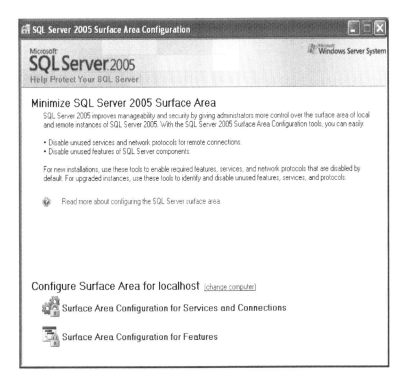

Click on

> *Surface Area Configuration for Services and Connections*

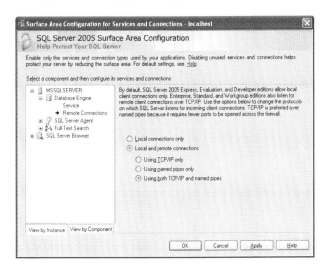

Expand the *Database Engine* and click on *Remote Connections*.

If the *Local Connections Only* radio button is selected, click on

➢ *Local and Remote connections*

➢ *Using both TCP/IP and named pipes*

➢ *Apply*

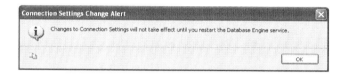

You will see a message warning you that the settings will not take effect until the database engine is restarted. To restart the database engine, click OK and select service.

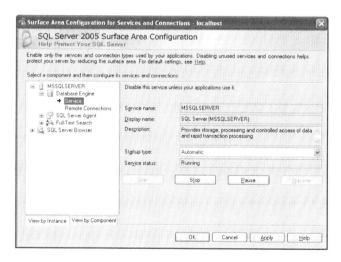

Then click the *stop* button, wait for the service to stop then click the *start* button.

Once the service has restarted, try the Telnet connection again. If it is successful the command prompt window will go blank. Close the command prompt and retry the connection test in BIRT.

If you have been successful you should see the Connection Successful confirmation.

You should now have a new data source available in the Data Explorer pane.

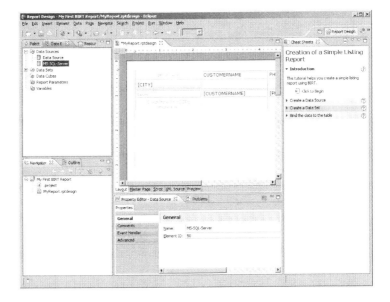

CREATE A DATA SET

The next thing to do is create a data set, this is essentially the table against which you want to report and it can be pre-filtered to show just certain records, plus you can add parameters into it which will be available to the viewer when running the report. You can create multiple data sets, even from multiple databases and then combine these to feed into a single report. But that comes under the heading of advanced and seeing as this is BIRT for Beginners start by creating a simple data set.

Create your data set by:

➢ *RIGHT CLICKING ON DATA SETS*

➢ *SELECTING NEW DATA SET*

and the following screen will be displayed.

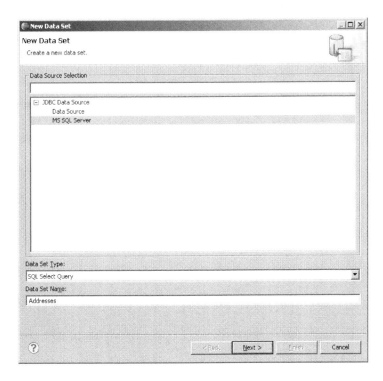

Select your data source from the list and enter a name for the data set – in my case I intend to list the addresses from my database, so I have called the data set "Addresses"

CLICK NEXT

Notice that the database users are displayed and under each user is a list of the tables that they have visibility over. Expand a table and the fields are listed.

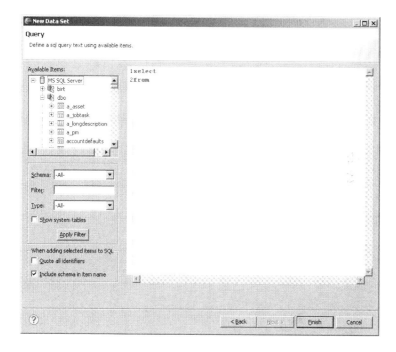

So in my case I expand the Address table to view the fields.

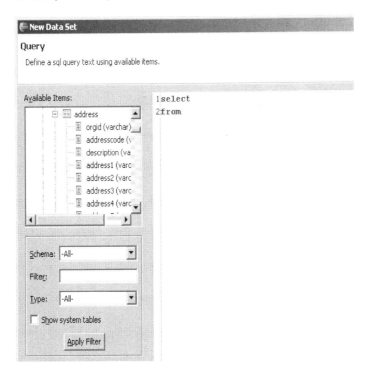

If you have a large database the filter function can be useful to limit the list of tables to certain schemas, types or custom filtered by name.

Once you have accessed the table you want you can start to drag fields into the familiar SQL select query on the right. When happy with your query click Finish.

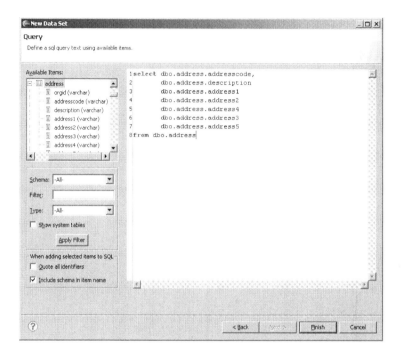

BIRT displays a screen where you can, amongst other things, see the results of your query.

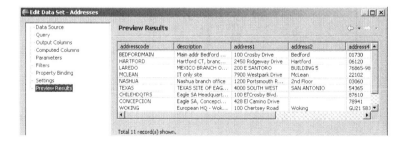

For now, just click OK and you will see that your data set is listed in the data explorer window.

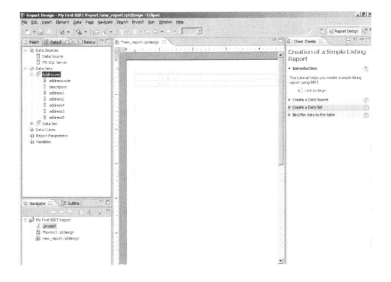

BUILDING THE REPORT

It is a simple matter of dragging fields from your data set into the table in the main body of your report to start to build up your report output.

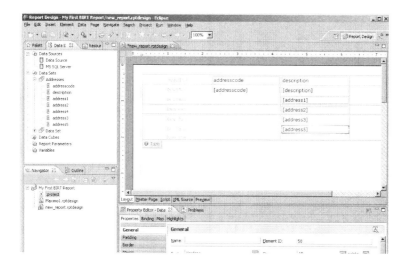

For now I have created a very simple example where I have inserted address lines in a column. To do this I had to create multiple detail lines, by right clicking on the left hand border of the table and selecting Insert/Row.

PREVIEW YOUR REPORT

Finally, it is time to preview the report which can be achieved by clicking on the fourth button from the left, in the toolbar.

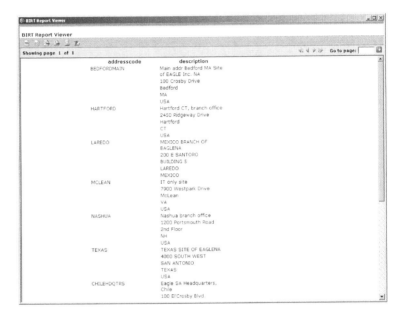

OK it's not very pretty and I will be looking at the format and styling options that BIRT provides a bit later, however this is enough to be going on with because now I want to focus on what you have to do to actually publish your report to a web browser.

PUBLISHING YOUR REPORT

In the Eclipse IDE, save your report to the default location (this is the location we selected during the BIRT installation) in my case C:\BIRT and remember this because you will need it later. I called my report *AddressReport.rptdesign*

To deploy or publish your reports you will need a web server, we will be using Tomcat, which you should have already downloaded by now, along with the required commons logging component and the BIRT runtime.

INSTALLING TOMCAT

On a Windows platform, simply run the *Apache-Tomcat-6.0.20.exe* installer and follow the wizard, selecting all the defaults.

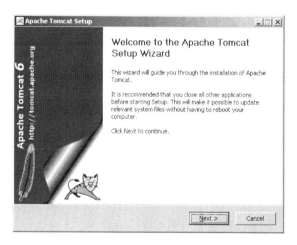

If you already have a version of Tomcat or another application that uses port 8080, then you may wish to change the port number during the installation.

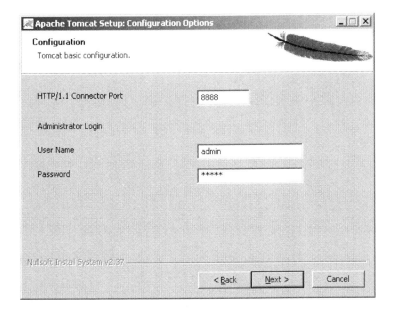

Also during the installation Tomcat will ask for the path to the Java virtual machine. This is the location where we installed Java to earlier and in my case it is

C:\Program Files\Java\jre6\bin

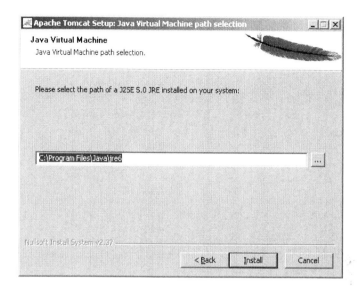

At the end of the installation you are prompted to start Tomcat.

Once this is done, to see if your Tomcat server is working simply open a web browser and point it at:

http://localhost:8888

Substituting 8888 in my example with the port that you selected during installation.

INSTALLING THE BIRT RUNTIME

Next unpack the *BIRT-Runtime-2_5_0.zip* into a temporary folder. Open the folder and locate the *WebViewerExample* folder. Copy this entire folder to the *WebApps* folder of the Tomcat installation.

E.g. C:\Program Files\Apache Software Foundation\Tomcat 6.0\webapps\WebViewerExample

and then rename the WebViewerExample folder to *BIRT-Viewer*

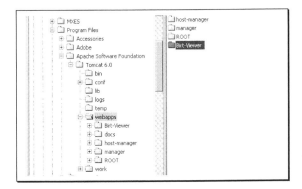

Next unpack the *commons-logging-1.1.1-bin.zip* and copy the contents of the Commons-logging-1.1.1 folder (note not the actual folder itself, just the contents) to:

C:\Program Files\Apache Software Foundation\Tomcat 6.0\webapps\BIRT-Viewer\WEB-INF\lib

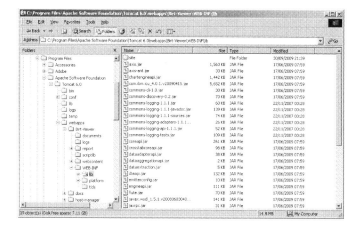

Now stop and restart the Tomcat server service. This step is important as without restarting Tomcat it will not pickup the changes you have just made!

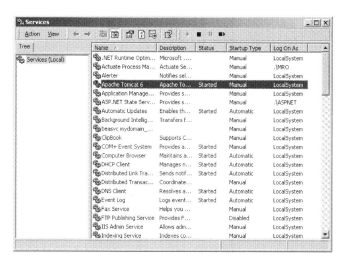

Now check that BIRT has been successfully installed into Tomcat. Point your browser at:

http://localhost:8888/manager/html

Remembering to substitute the 8888 with the port that you selected during Tomcat installation. If everything is working correctly you should be challenged for the username and password that you selected during the Tomcat installation and once through security you should see the following screen:

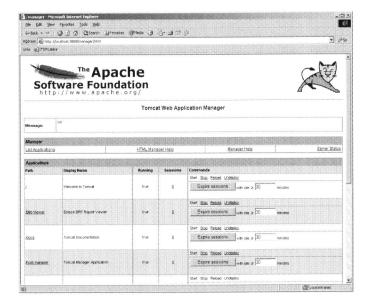

Click on the *BIRT-Viewer* link and you should see the following screen, confirming that BIRT is successfully installed.

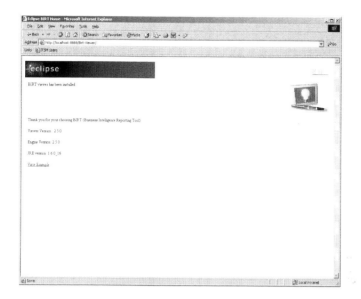

Now click on the *View Example* link and the following screen should be displayed, showing an example BIRT report in the web browser.

If you made it this far, give yourself a pat on the back and pop open a can of your favourite caffeinated fizzy drink!

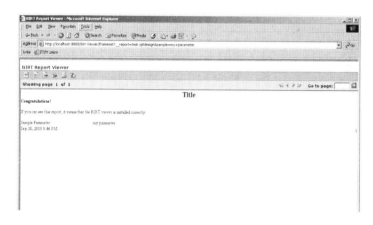

At this point, take a copy of the URL displayed in the browsers address bar, you will need it in a moment, the address in my case is:

http://localhost:8888/BIRT-Viewer/frameset?
report=test.rptdesign&sample=my+parameter

Now you need to move on to testing your own report that you created earlier. To do this you will need to make the JDBC driver available to Tomcat.

INSTALL DATA DRIVER FOR TOMCAT

Go to your downloads and open up the JTDS data driver and look for the *jtds-1.2.3.jar* file. This is the same file we copied earlier to the Eclipse folder. Copy it to

C:\Program Files\Apache Software Foundation\Tomcat 6.0\webapps\BIRT-Viewer\WEB-INF\platform\plugins\org.eclipse.BIRT.report.data.oda.jdbc_2.5.0.v2 0090605\drivers

If the *org.eclipse.BIRT.report.data.oda.jdbc_2.5.0.v20090605\drivers* folder does not exist, simply create it.

INSTALL YOUR REPORT UNDER TOMCAT

Now go and get the report you created earlier...

AddressReport.rptdesign

from the place you saved it to

e.g. C:\BIRT\ AddressReport.rptdesign

and copy it to the Tomcat web server, into the folder

C:\Program Files\Apache Software Foundation\Tomcat
6.0\webapps\BIRT-Viewer

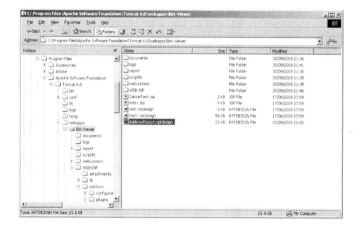

VIEW YOUR REPORT

Now point a browser at the address you used earlier to test your BIRT installation but replace the report name with the name of your report and strip off any additional parameters at the end of the address, so you end up with this address:

http://localhost:8888/BIRT-Viewer/frameset?
__report=addressreport.rptdesign

If your report doesn't work first time then try restarting the Tomcat server.

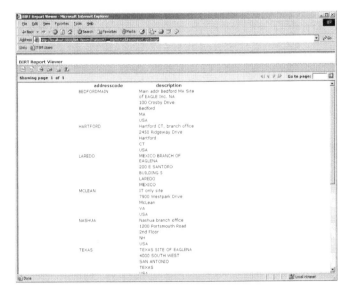

If you still have problems deploying your report then have a look at the Eclipse project web site where there are lots of tips and searchable error conditions to help you out.

http://www.eclipse.org/BIRT/phoenix/deploy/

SUMMARY OF GETTING STARTED WITH BIRT

Congratulations, by now you should have:

> ➤ Installed the BIRT report designer within the Eclipse IDE

> ➤ Followed the BIRT tutorials

> ➤ Connected BIRT with your own database

> ➤ Written a report against your own database

> ➤ Installed your web server

> ➤ Published your reports

SECTION 3

GETTING STARTED WITH ACTUATE BIRT

A beginner's guide to the commercial Actuate BIRT implementation. Here I cover how to download and install the software and create a well formatted listing report with a Flash chart whilst detailing solutions to some of the common problems you may find along the way. If you do not have the commercial version, this chapter is still worth a read because many of the techniques explained here are relevant to open source BIRT too.

ABOUT ACTUATE BIRT

So far we have experienced the open source version of BIRT. The next thing to do is download, install and play around with the demo version of the commercial Actuate implementation, to see how it differs, what had been added and importantly what benefits there are over the free version.

So here we start to compare the commercial implementation with the open source version and see just why we might want to spend good money on BIRT software.

As in the previous section I am going to walk you through how to get started quickly and expand on some of the concepts that we have seen before.

WHAT TO DOWNLOAD

At first I went to www.BIRT-exchange.com to see what I needed to download and immediately I noticed that there were several options available to me, which I found a little confusing from the off.

Ideally one big friendly download button would have been nice but it seems that Actuate have divided things up into a number of different packages for different purposes. So in order to find out what I needed I had to spend a while reading documents and trying to decide which version I should go for.

I like to get started quickly with software as there is so much rubbish out there and I want to either move forward or eliminate quickly so as not to waste valuable time with long downloads, installations and reading countless tutorials. Plus I don't want to spend too much time learning anything! Software should be intuitive and its use come naturally. However it seems that a bit of reading and learning is inevitable in this case and hats off to the Actuate marketing folks for creating just enough interest for me to move on at this stage and learn more about the product without giving up through information overload.

Clearly as a software author you want people to be invested in terms of time and knowledge in your products because this is what drives take up and usage and I can admit that Actuate seem to have the mix about right. Thankfully Actuate publish some good documents about the differences between the products in order to help you make your selection, I started off with this one:

http://www.BIRT-exchange.com/download/BIRT-Designers-Comparison-Table.pdf

I tend to like fully featured software, especially from a review perspective so I thought I would go for the option with "Professional" in the title, it also seemed to have a lot of ticks in boxes on the comparison chart! So tentatively I made and early stage decision to download the

Actuate BIRT Report Designer Professional

Next I noticed that I needed to select a BIRT deployment option, I wasn't sure what this was about because with my earlier investigation into Eclipse BIRT there was no such thing – you simply placed your completed reports on the web server. So again I needed to read through a document to understand what this was all about and make a choice.

Here is the headline text from BIRT-Exchange.com that introduces the subject:

Three products help execute and render BIRT reports. The BIRT Report Engine is a collection of Java classes and API's. The BIRT Deployment Kit is a lightweight Java EE report repository. BIRT iServer Express is a full-featured report server for scheduling and securing reports.

It appears that the major functionality provided by the deployment layer is to allow reports to be scheduled, have security applied and to be stored into personal repositories by end users. There were several options available and initially not wanting to go for something that had "server" in the title as this sounded like it will install huge amounts of software on my limited virtual PC, I eventually allowed curiosity to get the better of me and plumped for the Actuate iServer Express – at least it is an express version, which sounds like it will have a smaller footprint than the Enterprise version!

A little later on I discovered that I actually don't need a deployment solution in order to publish my reports as I can indeed simply put the reports I design with the Actuate designer into my Tomcat server and they will be accessible to my viewers. Well that's how it looks at the moment, we'll see!

Here's the comparison chart for the deployment options

http://www.BIRT-exchange.com/be/download/Deployment-Product-Comparison-Table.pdf

And finally I needed to select a viewer, no competition for this one, the whole thing that turned me on to BIRT in the first place was the very fancy ability it has to let users interact with the reports and only the top level viewer appears to offer all this functionality so the Actuate BIRT Interactive Viewer it is then! Here's the comparison chart...

http://www.BIRT-exchange.com/be/download/Viewer-Product-Comparison-Table.pdf

Whilst looking at these charts I noticed the costs associated with the various pieces of software. This stuff is not cheap! I am beginning to understand the rather clever marketing methodology behind Actuate's support of the Open Source BIRT project. It seems to be along the lines of "give away a lite version and sell the more advanced stuff". But no complaints there – I believe that software developers deserve to make a living and by producing these tools they help us to make a living and when you look at the costs of the kind of software that the advanced Actuate tools would be used with, it doesn't seem so costly after all.

To help you make your decision there are some video demonstrations available online. The quality between videos varies, some have audio, some don't, some played straight away and others didn't – that might just be my machine of course so see how you get on with them. Spending 30 minutes with the videos gave me a good overview and solidified my download decisions. The videos are available here:

http://www.BIRT-exchange.com/be/demos/all-demos/

Having been through the documentation I figured out that the Interactive Viewer is included with the iServer Express download, so ultimately all you need to download to get going is:

BIRT DESIGNER PROFESSIONAL

Design reports with Flash object support – 433 Mb

http://www.BIRT-exchange.com/be/downloads/BIRT-report-designers/?articleid=17321

ISERVER EXPRESS

For on demand and scheduled reports - 220Mb

http://www.BIRT-exchange.com/be/downloads/BIRT-deployment-options/

INSTALLATION

I started by running *ActuateBIRTReportDesignerPro.exe* and accepted all the defaults during the installation. Once the installation wizard was complete I launched the program from the Windows menu and it just worked! This is the first obvious benefit of using the Actuate package over piecing together all the pieces to install the Eclipse build.

DESIGNING YOUR FIRST REPORT

I'm pleased to say that the designer interface is pretty much the same as the one I am used to in the Eclipse BIRT implementation so I have already built up familiarity with this. In fact I am surprised at how much knowledge I have built up after only a few hours of using the Eclipse designer and that it is immediately transferable to this version, I was able to get started building a report very quickly.

CREATING A PROJECT

Initially I selected *File/New Project* and navigated to the Report Project option.

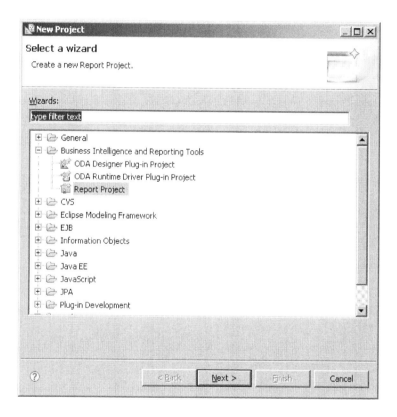

I named my project *"ActuateBIRTTest"*

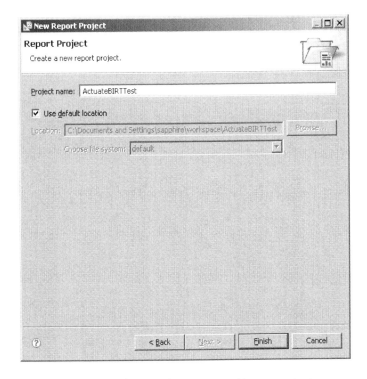

And just as expected my project appeared in my navigator.

CREATING A REPORT

Then I selected *File/New/Report* and named my report *ActuateTest.*

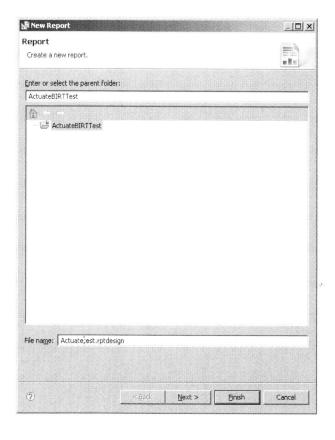

I was then presented with a list of predefined templates which seem similar to the Eclipse implementation

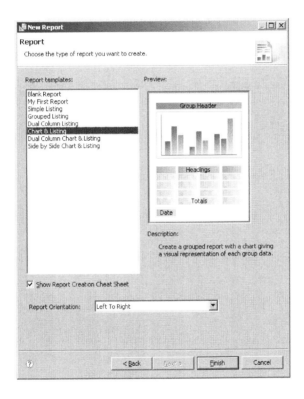

CREATING A DATA SOURCE

Next I selected *Data Sources*, right clicked and added a new data source

Now previously with Eclipse I had to download a JDBC driver for SQL Server, but… here I can select JDBC Data Source as a built in option. Again this is a nice touch over the Eclipse build.

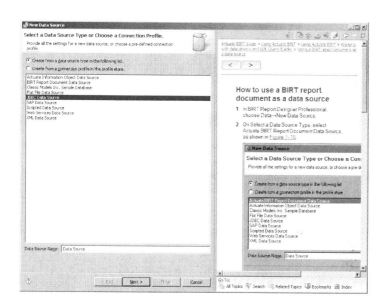

I referred to the online help during this process just to see how helpful it was and I am pleased to report that it is clear, easy to follow and detailed. I also love the way it is embedded into the currently open window.

Actuate have provided drivers for common data sources right out of the box, so no fiddling around to get my data driver set up. On selecting SQL server, the connection string was populated into the driver URL field waiting for me to specify my database and server details. This is such a small thing, but going back to use the Eclipse version later made me realise how useful it is to have the formatted string populated in advance.

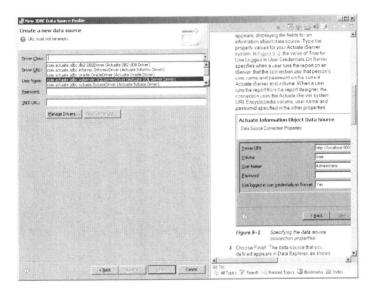

Here is the URL that I used to connect to SQL.

jdbc:actuate:sqlserver://localhost:1433;databasename=SUN5

CREATING A DATA SET

Next I created a data set by selecting *Data Sets / New Data Set* selecting the data source and providing a name for the dataset.

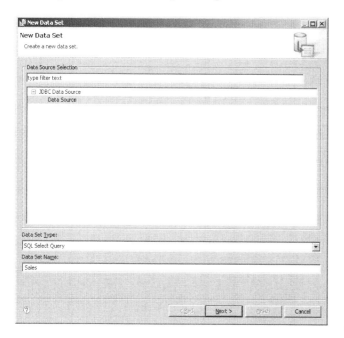

I was presented with the database table structure and faced the same problem as I did in the Eclipse build. Not all of my tables were available to me in the list. Luckily by now I had the solution which you can find in section 1 under "Connecting to SQL Server".

You may have noticed that the query builder here and in the Eclipse build is pretty basic. Whilst it is nice to have a full featured SQL query builder it really is not necessary. In the software that I produce I tend to save the cost of writing a dedicated query builder tool in favour of something simpler, exactly like BIRT does. The reason for this is that there are excellent SQL query builder tools available in Microsoft SQL server itself and other tools like Toad. So what I tend to do it use those tools to create my SQL, then copy it into here.

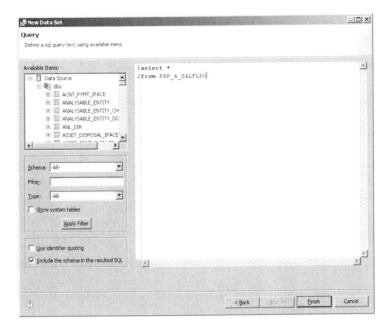

In this simple example I queried all the transactions in my financial ledger. This is quite a lot of data and would have made my report run quite slowly so I thought I had better apply a couple of filters, maybe by account code and accounting period, plus this gave me the opportunity to use the filter designer and see how well it worked.

APPLYING FILTERS

So I selected *Filter* from within the data source designer and was presented with a dialogue where I could select the field I wanted to filter on, presenting me with a list of fields looked up live, direct from my database. I was then able to select the operator, in this case *Greater than or Equal to.*

Next I needed to select the value to filter by and at this point I was thinking, "I have no idea what account codes exist in this database". I clicked on the value field and saw the option to *<Select Value...>,* clicking this made the software perform a live lookup on my database and present me with a list of my account codes. This is excellent as it really goes as far as possible in helping to create filters.

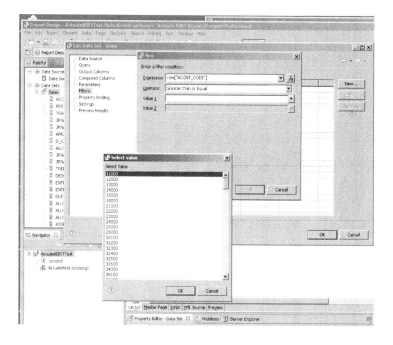

So far everything works just like it does in the Eclipse report designer, with a few extra nice touches that make the job just as easy as it possibly could be. For anyone who has an appreciation for databases and a rough idea of what they want to achieve this process is extremely straight forward.

ADDING DATA TO THE REPORT

Adding fields to the report works in the familiar Eclipse manner too, I simply dragged the accounting period, account code and description to my report table. At this stage I needed another column on my report for the value column and agreeably the designer is flexible enough to allow a column to be added on the fly.

One of the things I like about this way of doing it, over old Actuate and other report designers is that when you add a new column all the other columns are automatically resized to accommodate it. There is no fiddling around with moving fields and labels around by a pixel here and there to allow space for the new column to be inserted. So I selected the table, right clicked on the header cells and selected *insert/column to the right...,* then dragged my value field into that column.

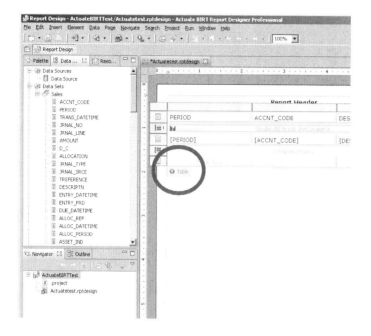

For insertion of groups, rows and columns, make the table design mode active by clicking anywhere in the table then clicking on the little table tab that appears at the bottom left.

GROUPING DATA

Now that I have my data on my report and filtered down to just my supplier codes, I need to group it by financial period and individual supplier within that.

So I right clicked on the table row header at the left of the detail table row and selected *insert Group.* I named the group *Period* and selected from the list of fields that was presented to me – usefully this is limited to just the fields appearing on the report.

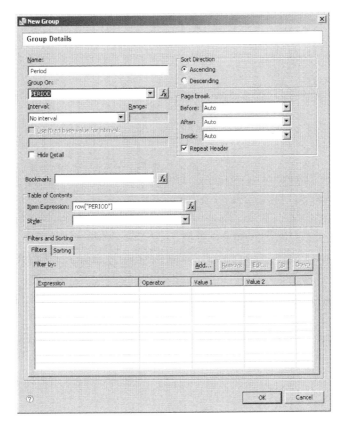

Obviously it makes sense to put the period value next to my period header so I simply dragged the field to that position

Next I followed the same procedure to insert an account group

AUGMENTING A DATA SET

I previewed my report and saw that it needed a bit of tidying up so I moved things around a bit and whilst doing this realised that I needed to add the account description to the report. This is held in another table on my database so I needed to find a way to add another table to an existing data set.

So I created a new data set called Accounts. Unfortunately I could not simply drag fields from this data set onto my report because I had not yet told Actuate how to link the data sets. So I had to create a third data set called *SalesByAccount*, which is a Joint Data Set, linking the two previous data sets by account code.

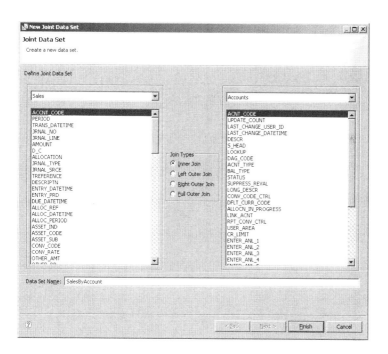

This shows the value in thinking carefully about your data sets before starting your report design, because I still could not drag fields even from my new data set onto the report. I actually had to unbind the table from the sales data set and rebind it to the *SalesByAccount* data set. This means of course some of the fields I had inserted onto the report so far were removed!

Unfortunately this didn't solve my problems either, I cant simply drag my fields onto my report as column bindings don't exist. So I decided to scrap my report table and start over based on the new data set.

Thankfully I hadn't done too much work so far and re-creating the report table was very easy to do. I dragged the Table object from the palette and it asked me about the table dimensions and source data set.

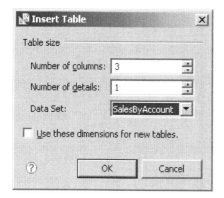

SIMPLE FORMATTING

Finally my report is starting to take shape, but I realise that I need to do a bit of formatting to make it look right.

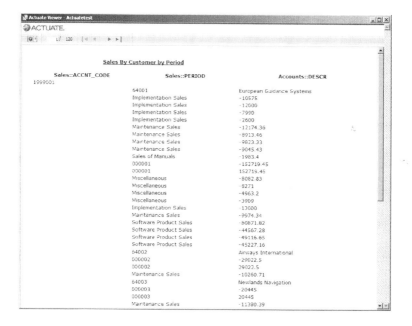

The first thing I do is increase the font size on the Period row and drop in a light blue background. I bolden the font on the customer row and drop in a slightly lighter background. This is all achieved by selecting the row by clicking on the left most cell in table design mode, then using the properties box at the bottom of the screen.

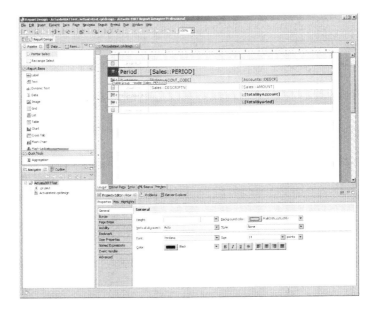

Finally, I use the Quick Tools Aggregate function from centre left of the design area to create a couple of sums in my two group footer areas. Naturally I colour the backgrounds and bolden the fonts. Then Insert a few spacer rows and we're done.

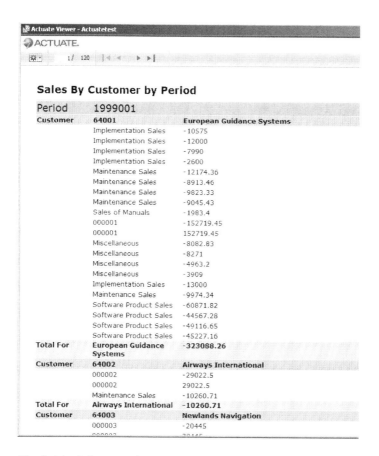

The finished, formatted report

FLASH CHARTS

Next I decided to get ambitious and insert a flash chart. Selecting from the objects palette on the left, and placing it in my report, the system automatically asked me if I wanted to download and install Adobe Flash Player. A nice touch.

On dragging my chart to the report layout I found that if I inserted it into the report above the table, it would not appear in the output. If I put it in a cell at the top of the table, then it was squashed up into the limited space available in the cell. So I highlighted the top row of cells used the right click and selected *"Merge Cells"*, this gave me a large single cell at the top of the page in which to insert my chart.

Having placed the chart object where I wanted it the chart dialog opened up and I was able to select my chart style.

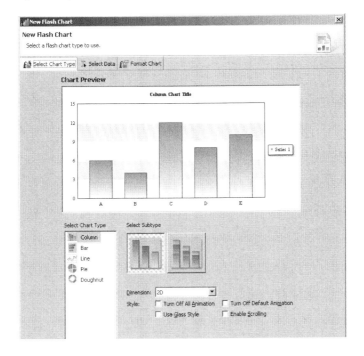

Next came the data selection. I noticed that it is possible to inherit the data from the area of the report where the chart was placed, or select one of my data sets, which means that I could theoretically have a chart based on summary level data and a detailed listing below. Since I want the chart to represent the data in the listing I selected to use data from my joined data set.

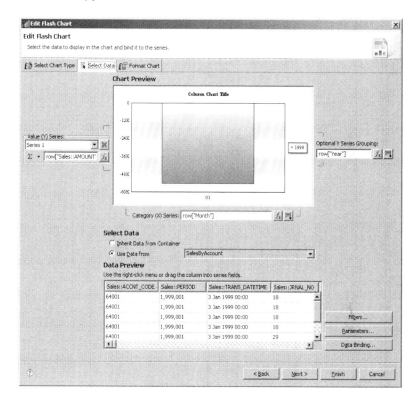

In this view it is possible simply to drag field headers from the data preview into the appropriate value or category series.

I want my chart to show sales value on the Y axis and time (months) on the x axis, for 1 year in total. This gave me two distinct problems!

1. My data set was not filtered by year, so in my first attempt at a chart I was seeing all sales for all years, the listing report was 120 pages long and the flash player kept popping up a message saying that the amount of data was causing the flash object to run slowly.

2. The period format in my database was 1999001 to represent January 1999, this clearly did not work because all I got at the bottom of the chart under columns 1 and two and so on was 19990011999002 – it looked awful!

To solve the first issue I needed to go back to my data set and filter the data so that only a single years worth of data was sent to the report.

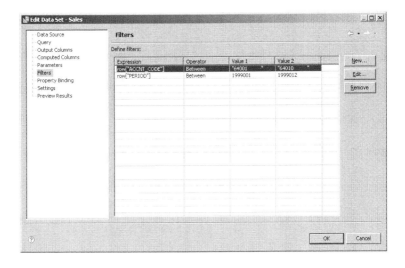

I did this on the sales data set, that made up one leg of my joined data set. Because then I was only feeding a single years worth of transactions into my joined data set, it caused the joined data set only to display a years worth of transactions.

I clicked on *New*, selected the field I wanted to filter on, selected the operator *"Between"* and then selected my value from and to range.

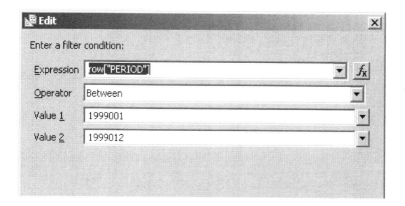

Problem 1 solved, my data was limited and so the chart would only be able to show a years worth of data.

Problem 2 was a little more tricky. The value 1999001 in my source data was an integer and I needed to perform a string operation on it. In other words I needed to chop off the left four characters to give me the year and the right 2 characters to give me the month. So I had to create an expression which first converted the integer to a string and then performed a left and right substring operation.

COMPUTED COLUMNS

For this I turned to the *Computed Columns* option in the data set and again used the expression builder to create my function. Because this was a slightly more complex function I opened up the expression editor by clicking on the *fx* button to the right of the expression box.

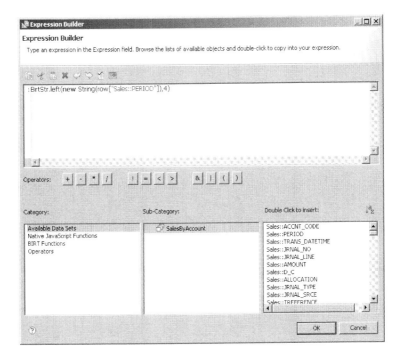

Here you can see how I have used the JavaScript *new String* function to convert the integer to a string and then wrapped it in the *BIRTStr.left* function to obtain the 4 left most characters of the string. All the fields and available functions are in the panels below the main expression window so it is easy to find the one you need.

So back to my chart, now I was able to grab the month and year fields and place them in the X series and optional Y series grouping fields to give me my months in numeric format along the bottom of the chart and my year in the legend box.

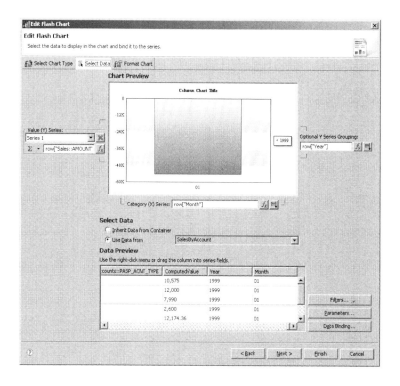

So far the report looks like this:

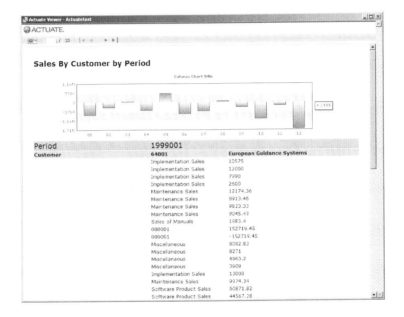

Another problem I had was that accounts systems are of course unfathomable to man or beast, this particular one stores my sales values as negative numbers! But I quickly sorted this out by adding another computed column which multiplied the sales value by -1 and presto my sales were (mostly) above the line!

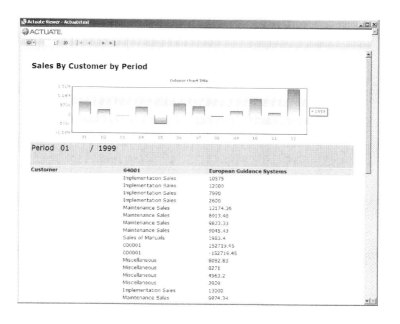

RUNTIME PARAMETERS

If you have a large data set you might like to offer your end user the opportunity to set filters on the range of data that is returned to their report. You can do this by adding run time parameters to the report, which are displayed to the user when they run it. The user can fill in the values they want and benefit from not having to wait while data they are not interested in is sent to their browser and also by not having to wade through pages of irrelevant data to get to the part they need.

To add parameters start by right clicking on the *Report Parameters* node in the data explorer and selecting:

>   *NEW*

>   *PARAMETER*

The Parameter dialogue is displayed.

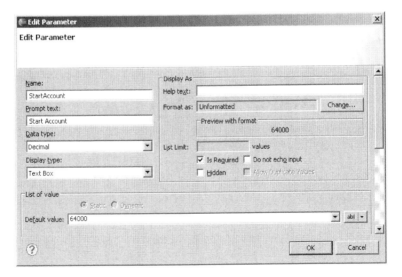

Here you start by naming your parameter and providing prompt text that will be displayed to the user, telling them what to enter. Next select a data type that matches the underlying database field that you will be filtering by the parameter. It is important to ensure the data type between the database and the parameter match, so if your database value is a decimal then your report parameter value should also be a decimal.

Finally select one of the display types from the list provided and optionally enter a default value.

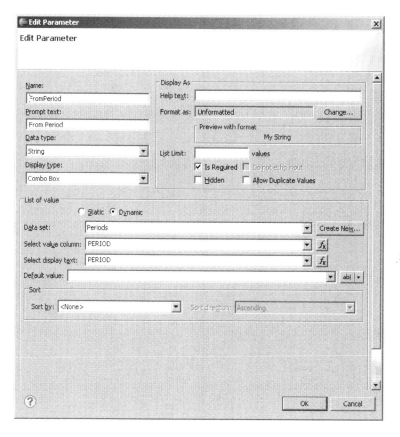

If you select a combo box (dynamic) at this stage, you can select the data set to display to the user, the value to select and the value to display. This means that you can provide the user with a dynamically looked up list of options to choose from and display an appropriate matching value from the table. For example, you could lookup an account code as a parameter but display the account name for the user to select from.

Note though, that you cannot select your dynamic combo values from the same table that is providing the data for your report, because that data set is filtered. No data will be returned from this data set until the parameters are provided and the parameters cannot be provided until they are looked up! The way around this is to create another unfiltered data set and provide the combo values from this.

In our example I am reporting on the Transactions data set (which is parameterised to filter between a range of periods). I create another data set called periods, which selects a distinct period value from the transactions table, then build my parameter combo boxes from this data set.

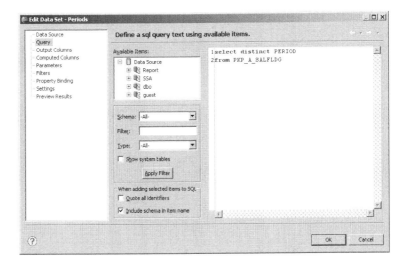

Do this for as many display parameters as you need, then go on to setting up the parameters on your queries. Right click a data set and select *Edit*

Open the Query section and add a where clause to range the data by the parameters that you require. In this example we are ranging between 2 financial periods. Use a question mark to indicate each parameter that is to be replaced at runtime.

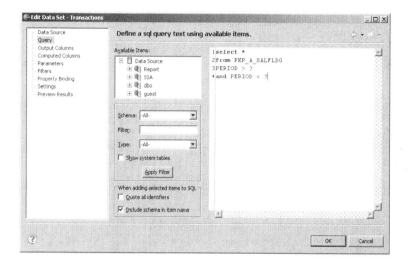

Next click the Parameters option and you will see that the parameters have been inserted for you, based on the number of question marks that you entered earlier.

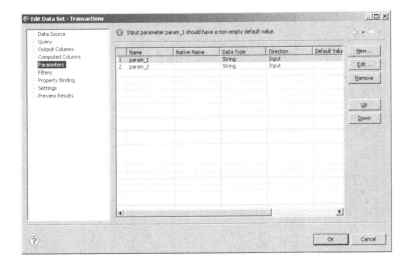

Click on each parameter and click *Edit* to display the parameters dialogue.

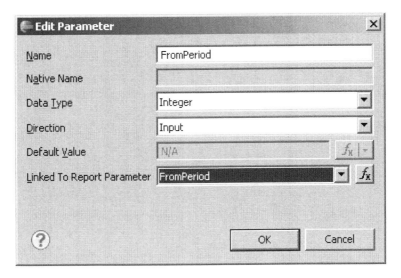

Rename the parameter, select the data type, leave the direction as input and link it to a report parameter from those that you created earlier. Do this for all your parameters.

Now when you run the report, you are able to select the to and from parameter values before the limited data set is fetched from the server.

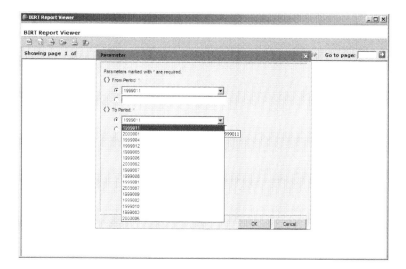

It is possible to add many parameters to a report and have them based on any data set or joined data set that you like, so there is a lot of power hidden behind this seemingly simply piece of functionality. In the end it allows you to provide usability for your end users and importantly let them decide on the data ranges that they need to see.

Reports that return large data sets from the server will inevitably take longer to run than those that return lower volumes and summarised data, so by filtering on parameters the user can often get to their results faster. This is worth considering at design time, to avoid complaints later from your users, about the report being slow to run!

SUMMARY OF GETTING STARTED WITH ACTUATE BIRT

If you have been following these examples you should have

➢ Created a simple listing report

➢ Created a joined data set

➢ Added some filtering

➢ Added parameters

➢ Added data manipulation

➢ Inserted a flash chart object

Having already used many of these techniques in the open source version it was very easy to accomplish this simple report and those features that I had not previously used were intuitive to understand.

So far it is easy to see that the commercial Actuate implementation over the open source Eclipse build adds a few nice touches but quite possibly not enough to justify the expenditure.

Where it really gets interesting is in the deployment options. Once you have created your reports these are quite limited when using the open source implementation and this is an area where Actuate have made some big improvements. This can make real business sense to companies that choose to implement this technology and the commercial additions to BIRT are well worth looking into.

SECTION 4

ISERVER EXPRESS AND THE INTERACTIVE BIRT VIEWER

Continuing our journey into BIRT Reporting we install the iServer Express, find an excellent online guide and follow it to view reports, modify reports and save the modified versions in our own user area on the iServer.

ABOUT ISERVER & THE INTERACTIVE VIEWER

So far we have looked at how to easily get started with the Open Source (free of charge) version of BIRT and then moved on to compare some of the differences between that and the Actuate commercial version.

In this section we take a look at two of the additional commercial components, the iServer Express and the BIRT Interactive viewer.

Having been able to easily create and run reports on my web server using the open source products I was a little confused as to what else the additional product offerings could do for me and in this section we find out.

One point I would like to mention at this stage, is that many people I have been speaking to recently about BIRT tell me that they are too short of time to spend enough time learning and getting to know BIRT. I understand the time pressures people are under and one of the things that has impressed me the most about BIRT is how quickly I have been able to learn a surprising amount about it. All you need to do it give yourself a few hours a week and follow these guides and you will be up and running in no time. Often the hardest step on any journey is the first, so put a note in your diary, block out an hour of time this week to spend in the company of this wonderful report writer and see where your journey takes you!

Staying with the subject of time shortages for a moment, one of the great things about iServer Express is the fact that it is a tool that is designed to save you time. Having been involved with many organisations with fairly large user communities I can't help but notice that users' demands for reports can eat time away from the IT department like it is going out of fashion. Also, with so many reports and variations of reports floating around an organization in different formats and created using different tools this is an area that is quite difficult to keep track of easily.

iServer Express solves both of these problems by allowing you to publish your reports to a central location that is available to the whole organisation or selected users depending on their security permissions. This keeps all the reports in one place and means that you can easily direct a user to the correct location when they need that urgent report.

Also, after a while you will have built up quite an impressive report repository on the iServer so the majority of users last minute urgent request should be able to be met by a report from your library. Sometimes of course you might have to make small amendments to one of your standard library reports in order to meet a specific request. This is where iServer Express lends you another helping hand as the user can select a report which is similar to what they need and then make their own minor modifications to it using the Interactive Viewer, then save the modified version into their own personal report library.

Great for the end user because they don't have to depend (and wait) on someone from IT to create their report for them and great for IT because the number of end user report modification requests drops significantly.

Once again, Actuate have clearly put some thought into this product and are solving actual user's real world problems in an easy to learn and quick to implement technology solution.

DOWNLOADING THE SOFTWARE

If you have been following the previous chapters of this book you will already have downloaded the iServer Express and Interactive Viewer installer package. But as a reminder you can get this from here:

Select option 3 with iServer express – 220 Mb

http://www.BIRT-exchange.com/be/downloads/BIRT-report-viewers/?articleid=17323

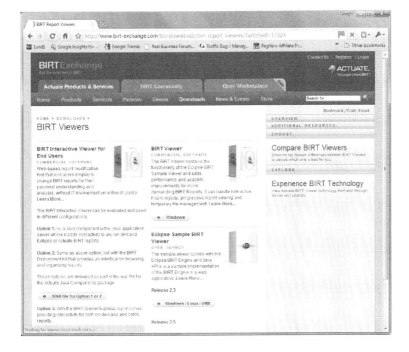

ISERVER EXPRESS INSTALLATION

As with the Actuate BIRT designer professional the installation was very straight forward. I just ran the installer package and followed all the defaults. There are a few settings that you may need to change depending on your server configuration but I would recommend that for your first attempt you run this up on a virtual machine and just go with the default settings.

The installer is a simple exe called:

ActuateiServer Express.exe

It will place 3 icons on your desktop:

iServer 10 Getting Started Guide

iServer Management Console 10

iServer Express 10

STARTING THE ISERVER

The iServer Express 10 shortcut is the one to start with and this will launch the iServer Express login screen. You can also launch a web browser and go to the following address:

http://localhost:8900/iportal

Naturally if you are logging on remotely then substitute localhost with the name of your server.

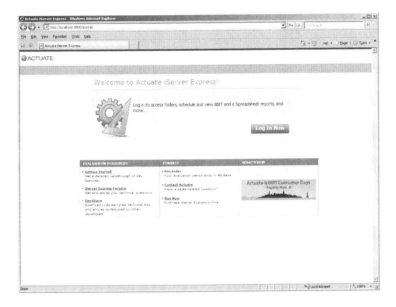

Hit the *Log in Now* button and when prompted enter the user name *Administrator* and leave the password blank

FAMILIARISATION

It is worth spending a few minutes familiarising yourself with the layout of the main screen.

On the left you will see the "report tree" which starts with your server name at the very top. Under this in the Documents folder is your home folder and within this your personal folder. You are logged in as the Administrator so that is the name of your personal folder. This is the location where you will save your personal reports to and each user gets their own personal area. You can always jump to your personal folder by pressing the "My Folder" link at the top right of the screen.

Next is the public folder where reports are stored for all users.

When you select a folder, you will see it's contents displayed on the right as a list of reports and to the right of each report are a series of icons, hover your mouse over them to see what they do. We will be using the 2nd one in from the left in a moment.

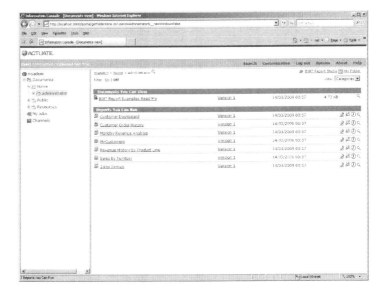

To start with navigate to:

Public / BIRT and BIRT Report Studio Examples.

And open the Customer Dashboard report

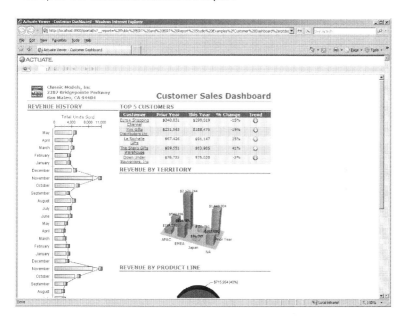

You will see that it pops open a new browser window containing the report. Feel free to have a look at some of the other reports while you are here.

MODIFYING AND SAVING A REPORT

Launch the Sales by Customer report, but this time, don't just click the link, but click the second icon in from the left in the little group of icons that live on the right of the report title.

When you hover your mouse over it you will see the description *"Run on Demand and Save Results"*

This will launch the Save As window, where you can select which folder to publish to and give the document a name and version. For now just modify the name slightly to something that you will recognize later and press Finish.

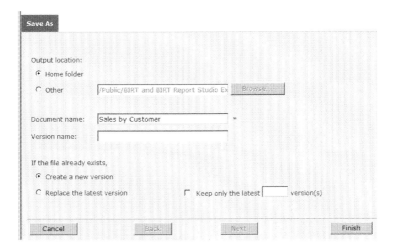

INTERACTIVITY

When the report is displayed try moving through the pages using the CD style buttons at the top left to get a feel for how these work.

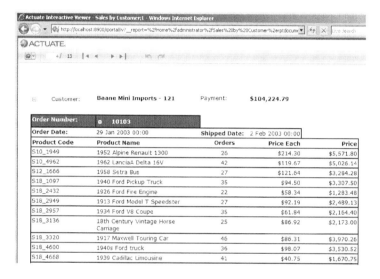

Next enable interactivity on the report by clicking on the "cog" button at the top left of the report and selecting

Enable Interactivty.

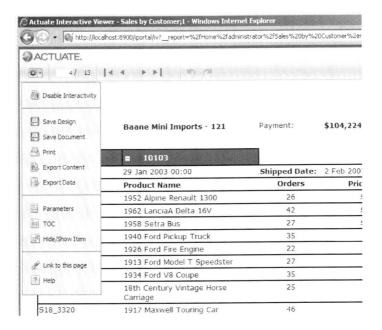

Immediately you will see little "-" signs appearing on the report. These allow sections of the report to be "Collapsed" and expanded again.

Also, by right clicking on any column of the report you can see a context menu that allows you to do various things.

Try hiding a column by selecting

Column / Hide Column

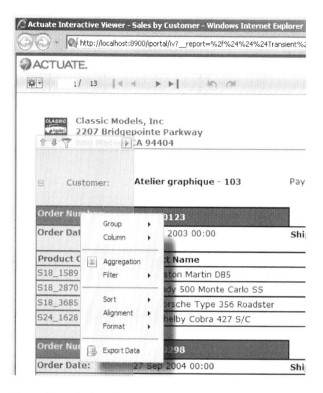

Then show the hidden column by right clicking anywhere in the report and selecting Column / Show Column and selecting the column name from the window that appears. Try playing around with the various options, don't be shy because it is impossible to break anything, as you can simply close the report and run the original again. Here are a few of the things you can do in interactive mode:

> Add calculations and aggregations to columns

> Apply filters to the report data

> Modify the way the report groups data

> Sort the report by any column

> Modify fonts, number formats and text alignment

Next, open up the *"Product Sales by State"* report, again using the "Run on Demand and Save Results" button. You will notice that this one asks you for a parameter.

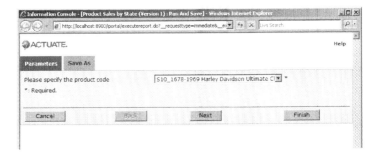

Select a value then click the *Save As* tab, provide a new name for the report and click *Finish*.

This report has a chart at the top, enable interactivity, right click the chart and click Format Chart.

This quick example demonstrates that the users can even change the chart type at runtime!

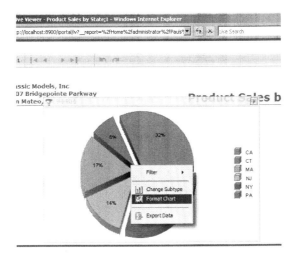

After playing around with this a bit go back to the report tree and look in the Home/Administrator folder and you should see your saved reports with the slightly different names you gave them earlier.

SUMMARY ISERVER EXPRESS & INTERACTIVE VIEWER

The iServer Express is a nice add-on to the BIRT implementation and it is easy to see how it can deliver real value, efficiencies and time savings over the tool set that is available purely as open source.

It is also intuitive and easy to use so once you have it up and running why not make it available to a small sample of your user community and see how they get on?

If you produce software that uses BIRT as it's primary reporting tool, then the iServer Express and Interactive Viewer tools can add value to your end users.

SECTION 5

DESIGNING INFORMATION OBJECTS

In the next two sections we look at how to allow end users the ability to create and run their own reports over the web, whilst retaining data access under the control of IT. First we look at how to create data Information Objects that present a unified and normalized view of your data to the end users.

ABOUT INFORMATION OBJECTS

After having reviewed the freely available open source BIRT report designer and deployment options as well as the Actuate designer and iServer Express we are taking things a step further by looking at the Actuate BIRT Studio. This promises to allow end users the capability to design their own reports, over the web, whilst still being within the control of the IT department.

Actuate BIRT Studio is a commercial product and is available in a number of options. Essentially these are:

1. As a java component that you can deploy into your own application server e.g. Apache Tomcat

2. As part of an end user report writing portal, which basically includes a deployment kit and saves you the time and effort of creating your own deployment environment.

3. As an extension to the iServer Express, allowing users to schedule their own reports in the iServer environment.

For full details and pricing see the Actuate BIRT-Exchange website page here...

http://www.BIRT-exchange.com/be/products/BIRT-report-designers/actuate-BIRT-designer-for-end-users/features/

Or for some assistance in navigating the pricing and deployment options contact BIRTReporting.com, where we offer a full range of implementation and training solutions.

In order to allow users to create their own reports you first need to publish data sources for them to base their reports on. In Actuate these are called Information Objects, the name reflecting the fact that you are not exposing users to raw database tables and fields, but rather a set of tables and fields that you have prepared for them.

MULTIPLE SYSTEM REPORTING

An Information Object can contain data from several different sources. So long as there is a common field to link the independent data sources you can specify as many as you like, meaning that you can offer users data from different systems in a single unified view!

CLEAN DATA VIEWS

Once you have selected the basis for the data sources you can then rename fields so as to provide the user with field names that make sense to them in business terms, rather than in database terms. So if you have fields in your database such as AD_CD_1 (which might mean Address Code 1) you could rename this to Primary_Address_Code for example.

You can also remove fields that the end user would have no interest in. For example any index fields or fields that simply exist to relate one record to another can be removed from the end user view.

Finally you can add filters and grouping to the data, so for example if you have a large transaction table you could filter it by month or year, to provide sets of transactions that the user could select based on the type of report they want to create.

END USER WEB BASED REPORT DESIGN

Once you have created a series of Information Objects you can hand the job of creating reports over to your end user community. The report designer presents a clean, easy to understand and intuitive design environment to the end user directly in their web browser with no further software to install.

I will be covering designing reports in the next section aimed fairly and squarely and end user report designers, so if you decide to implement BIRT Studio you can provide a copy of the PDF version of this section (available online at http://www.BIRTReporting.com) to your users as a startup guide.

WHAT TO DOWNLOAD

The demo download is a hefty 157 Mb and can be obtained from here:

http://www.birt-exchange.com/be/products/birt-report-
designers/actuate-birt-designer-for-end-users/features/

USING ISERVER EXPRESS

If you have been following the examples in this book, you will already have downloaded the iServer Express package, which contains the studio as an add-in to the iServer Express. If you want to get started straight away then open up iServer Express in your web browser, log in and launch the BIRT Report Studio from the link at the top right.

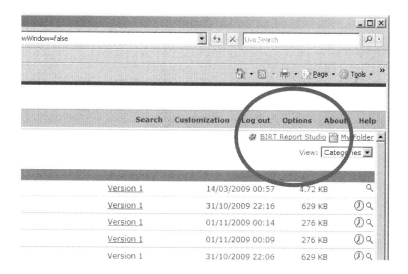

INSTALLING INTO TOMCAT

If you don't wish to use the iServer Express then you need to install the Java components into an application server.

Locate the Tomcat WebApps folder, in a default installation this is:

C:\Program Files\Apache Software Foundation\Tomcat 6.0\webapps

Now open up the ActuateJavaComponent_war.zip file and copy the ActuateJavaCompenent.war file to the WebApps folder.

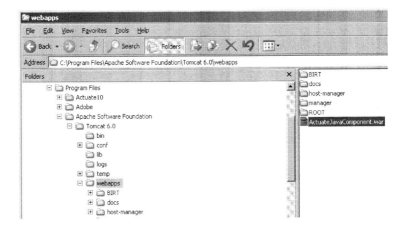

Now go to *Control Panel/Administrative Tools/Services* and restart the Tomcat server.

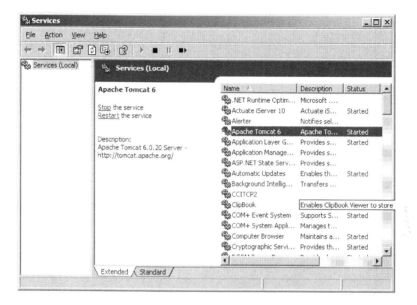

You should see that an ActuateJavaComponent folder is created.

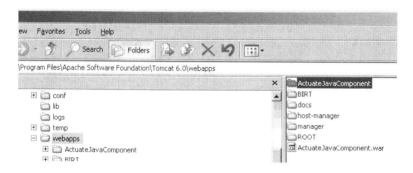

Note: if you have already installed the iServer Express then the service to stop and start is called Actuate iServer 10 and the default installation folder is:

C:\Program Files\Actuate10\iServer\servletcontainer\webapps

Now launch your web browser and point it at:

http://localhost:8888/ActuateJavaComponent/

The components overview screen should appear. Click on Actuate BIRT Report Studio, then again on the following page to launch the report studio.

The BIRT Report Studio opens in the web browser.

Click New to start a new report

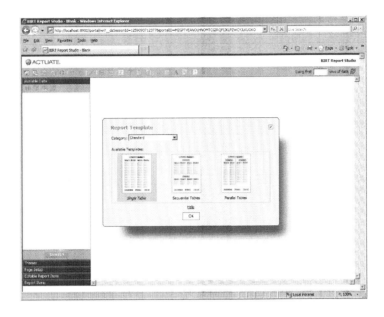

Select a template from the available options. For now go with the simple table option, there's always time to get more adventurous later!

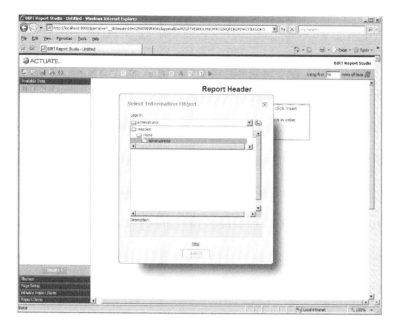

You will now be presented with a directory selection from where you can select an Information Object. We have not yet created an Information Object, so for now just familiarise yourself with the directory structure – in my case this is

MSADEM/Home/Administrator

CREATING AN INFORMATION OBJECT

Now we can get to creating an Information Object to provide data to the report studio. An Information Object presents your underlying data to the user in a way that is appropriate to their skill level and interest level.

Business users are not usually database experts and so they want a user friendly view of the data. This is what an Information Object provides. Information objects are powerful things and can hold data from a variety of different sources. So for example you can use a data object to provide a base for reports that work across multiple systems!

A key tip for creating data objects is to keep them simple. Present too much data in a single Information Object and it will only serve to make the system look complicated to the end user.

Start the BIRT Report Designer Professional and select

File / New / Project

Then select *Information Object Project* from the dialogue that appears.

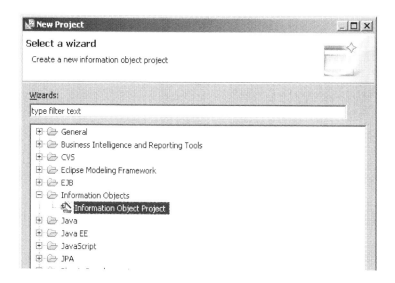

Click Next and give the project a name

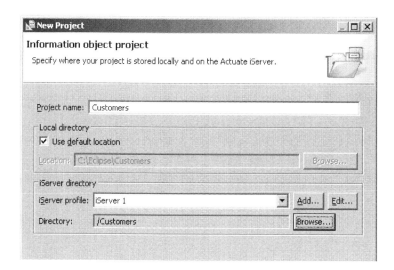

Now we need to create an iServer profile, essentially connecting our Information Object to the iServer. If you have a profile already simply select it from the drop down menu, otherwise press the Add button. The default values should be fine but do ensure that you use the correct ports that you selected when installing the iServer.

Next hit the browse button and navigate to the directory that you made a note of when defining a new report in the BIRT Report Studio. In my case this was: MSADEM/Home/Administrator

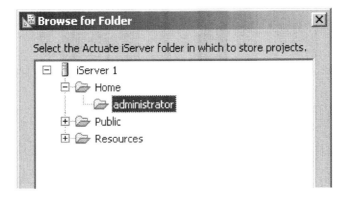

Click OK and Finish. The system may ask you if you wish to open the IO Design Perspective, since this is the Eclipse perspective that we will be using to create our Information Object, click Yes.

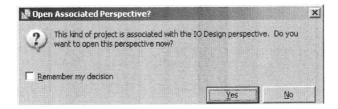

The IO Design Perspective opens and your project is available in the Navigator pane.

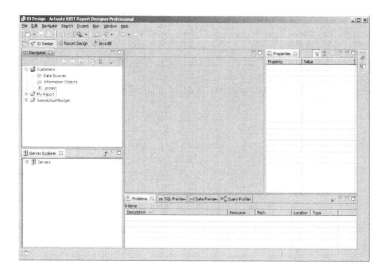

CREATE A DATA CONNECTION DEFINITION

Right click on your project's Data Sources folder and select

New / Data Connection Definition

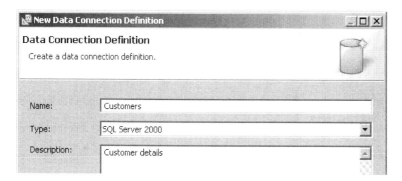

Don't worry about the configuration key, just click Finish, then in the screen that appears complete the database connection details. Notice that your data connection is saved on the left as as a .dcd file, in my case, Customers.dcd

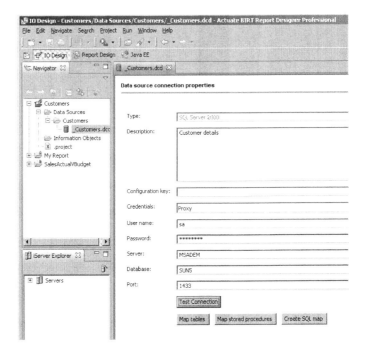

Click Test Connection to see if your connection details are correct.

Next click the Map Tables button to display the mapping screen.

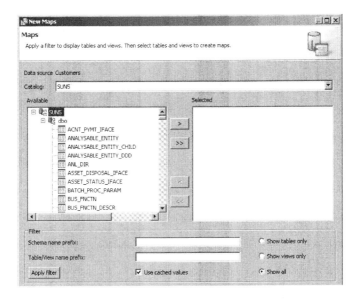

If the list of tables does not appear, click the *Apply Filter* button and wait a few seconds for it to refresh.

Double click on the tables you want to include in your data connection so that they move over to the right hand side, then click finish.

You should end up with a screen showing you the fields in the table you selected. Also notice how the map file (sma) is displayed in the customers folder on the left hand side.

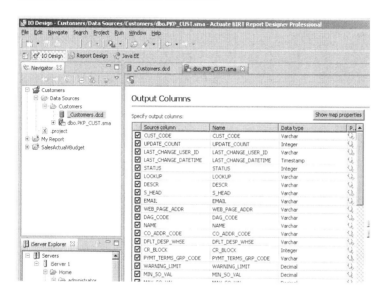

Now click on the refresh button in the data preview tab at the bottom of the screen, wait a few seconds and you should see the data from the table appearing.

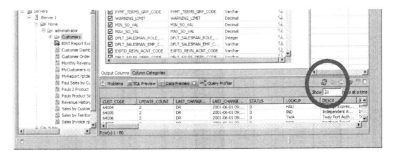

You can create as many maps as you need, from your single data source. In my case my customer addresses are in a separate database table, so I created a map called addresses, by right clicking on my customers folder and selecting *New / Map*.

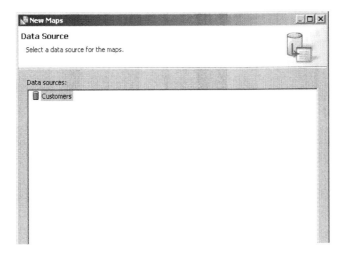

When you create a new map in this way you are presented with a list of your data sources to choose from and then walked through the same procedure as before, to select the table.

Next right click on Information Objects in the navigator and select

New / Information Object, give it a name and click Finish.

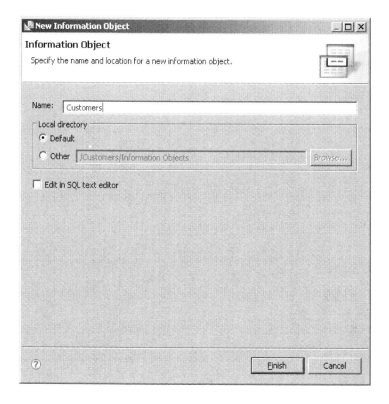

Now you should see the Information Object Designer screen.

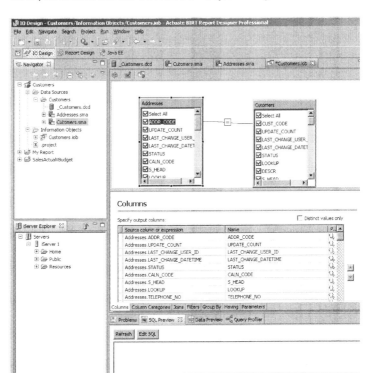

To build your Information Object simply drag the data sources (map files), in my case Addresses and Customers into the main window and link them by dragging the related field from one table to the related field in the other. A line will be drawn between the tables.

Click the refresh button as before to ensure that your Information Object returns the data you are expecting.

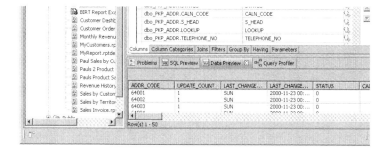

PUBLISH THE INFORMATION OBJECT

Select the Information Object project (at the top of the navigator tree view) and click *File / Publish*

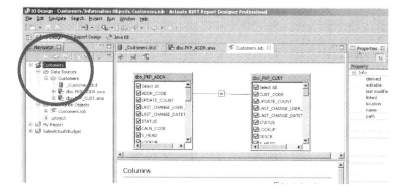

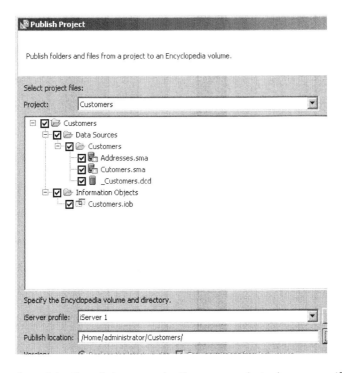

Complete the dialogue as in the screen shot above, specifying the iServer profile and the publish location. This should be the same location you identified earlier. Then click *Publish Files.*

CONNECTING THE REPORT TO THE INFORMATION OBJECT

Now it's time to go back to the BIRT Report Studio and if you have not done so already, close the Select Information Object dialogue, then re-open it and navigate to the Information Object that you have just published.

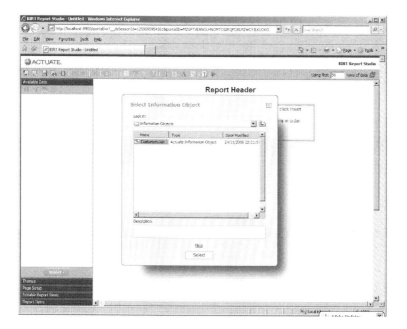

This time you will see the fields from your data Information Object listed, ready for you to use.

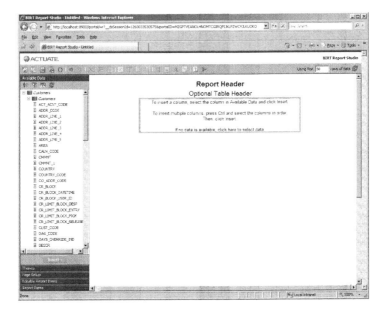

You are now ready to start building your report, of course at this point you could hand the job of creating reports over to your end users as everything from this point on can be achieved directly in the web browser!

The next section covers this in detail and is purposely seperate from this section so that you can use the accompanying PDF copy, available from BIRTReporting.com, as a guide to give to your end users.

For the remainder of this section we will look at making modifications to the Information Object.

RENAMING & DELETING DATABASE FIELDS

We have seen how we can present data from different tables (and using the same principal from different databases) to an end user as a unified data source. This allows them a simplified and logical view of the data sources. One of the additional benefits of providing Information Objects to users is the ability of an Information Object to rename the original database fields to a more end user friendly name.

For example, in my database I have fields called ADDR_CODE & CMMNT. This is not a bad naming convention and it is pretty obvious what the fields contain, however not all databases are as well defined as this one. For the purposes of this example I am going to show you how to rename the fields to more user friendly names.

Go back to your Information Object designer and open up the iob file.

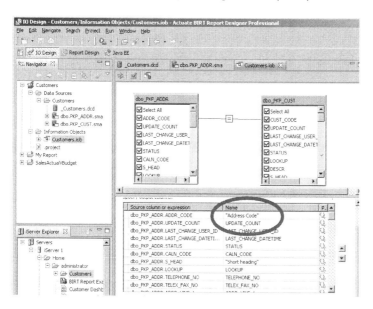

Now simply type the user friendly names for any of the fields in the Name column. To delete fields simply highlight the field you want to delete and click remove.

FILTERING AND GROUPING

If you have a large data set you may wish to add filters so that not all the data is served up to the end user. Serving up large data sets over the web can take time and this would result in the inevitable complaints that the reporting system is slow to respond. The key to avoiding this type of complaint is to filter the data at source into discreet and logical subsets that the user may wish to use.

To add a filter use the filters tab at the bottom of the Information Object window. Select New and use the standard query builder to add your filters.

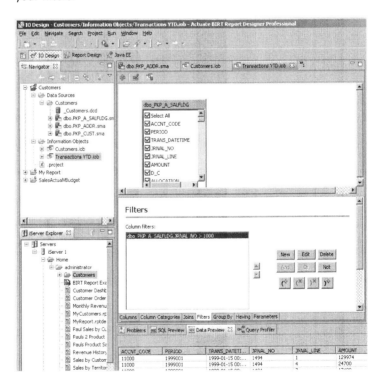

Once you have finished cleaning up the field names go back to the report designer and hit the refresh button. You will see that the new clean and lean field names appear.

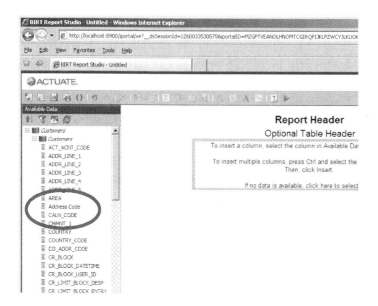

Here is our renamed Address Code field seen from the end users point of view in the BIRT Report Studio.

SUMMARY DESIGNING INFORMATION OBJECTS

In this section we have looked at how to create an Information Object against which your end users can create their own reports in a completely web based environment.

A little thought about the design of your Information Objects in terms of which tables they contain, how those tables are joined and filtered and how the field names are modified to present an understandable view to your end users will pay dividends in the long run.

Your end users should be able to understand and appreciate the data sets that you provide them with and if you can create your Information Objects in this way then you will gain the full benefits of this paradigm.

There is one way to ensure that you produce the right kind of Information Objects for your users and that is to ask them what they need. In the registered users area of BIRTReporting.com there is a downloadable PDF sample form that you can use to publish to your end users for this very purpose. Registration is free of charge for readers of this book.

SECTION 6

WEB BASED REPORT DESIGN

Design, publish, maintain and run your own reports entirely over the web. In this section we look at the Actuate BIRT Report Studio and walk through creating your first report in the web browser.

ABOUT WEB BASED REPORT DESIGN

This is a quick start guide to using the BIRT (Business Intelligence Reporting Tools) Report Studio.

The BIRT Report Studio allows you to create reports in your web browser with an easy to use, intuitive drag and drop graphical interface. The reports you create can contain multiple listings. Graphs, sums and groups and can be saved for later retrieval and viewing by yourself or other users of the system.

The reports you create are based on data that your IT department makes available to you. The fundamental selection of data provides sets and subsets of data which you can then use to create many different reports.

You can specify what data the IT department should make available to you and we have published an example form for this purpose on the BIRTReporting.com web site. Use it as an example and feel free to modify it to suit your individual requirements. The only thing we ask is that you maintain the copyright message on the form and send us a copy of any modified forms you create so that we can make them available to the wider user community. Naturally you will need to remove any business sensitive information from any forms you send to us for publication.

OPENING THE REPORT DESIGNER

This is most easily achieved by following the link that your IT department will provide, however if you are using the iServer Express then you will find a link to BIRT Report Studio at the top right of the screen.

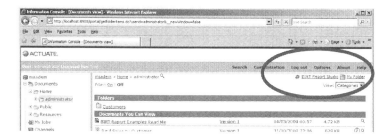

Enter your username and password to log in and you will see the starting page inviting you to open and existing report or create a new one.

STARTING A REPORT

Select New to start a new report

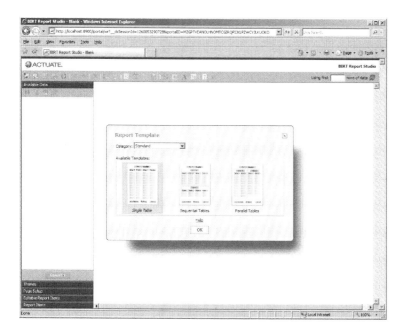

You will see a screen with several templates. Select a template and click OK.

The next screen you see will allow you to select a data set on which to base your report.

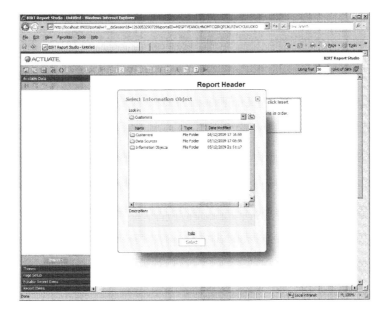

Look for the Information Objects folder and from within it select an appropriate data set.

Having selected a data set the main report design screen will open and you will see a list of the fields available to you in the left hand pane.

In our example we are looking at a list of transactions from our accounting system and the transactions have been linked to the customer name and address fields. For our example report we are going to produce a listing of transactions by customer by accounting period, showing the per period and per customer balance.

ADDING FIELDS TO THE REPORT

Adding fields can be achieved in 3 ways.

Either double click on the fields you wish to add, or hold down the control key and click multiple fields, then click the Insert button, or finally drag the fields you want to use into the main body of the report. Don't worry about where you drag them as BIRT will automatically create a table for you and insert the fields either to the left or right of existing columns.

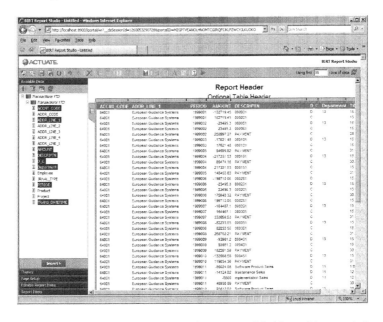

For our example we have selected a range of fields and inserted them into the report.

MERGING COLUMNS

In our data set we have an account code and an account name. We want to merge these into a single column to keep the report tidy. To do this, we hold down the control key whist clicking on the columns we wish to merge. The columns do not have to be adjacent. You will see that the selected columns are indicated with a light blue border.

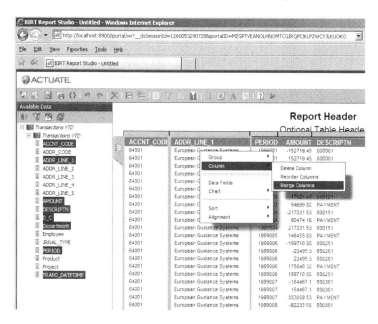

We can then right click anywhere in the selected columns and select *Column/Merge Columns*

The result is that the selected columns are merged into one. Don't worry about the headings for now, we can tidy those up a bit later.

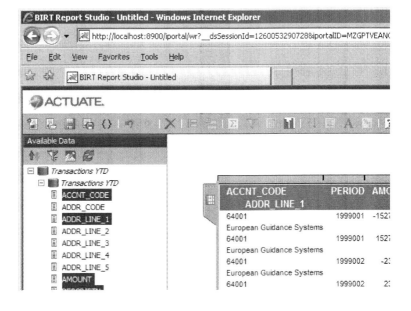

GROUPING DATA

We wish to group our data by customer and by accounting period. To achieve this first we select the customer column and then either right click and select Group / Add Group, or select the group button from the toolbar and then click on the add group button that appears.

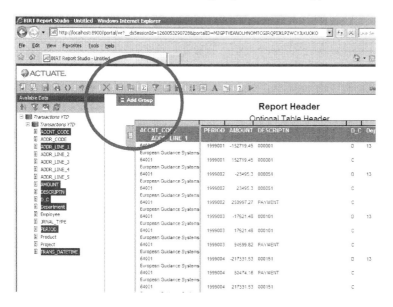

A dialogue will appear asking you which field you wish to group by.

Select the field and click apply.

You will notice that it is only possible to press the group button for one field at a time and not a merged column which contains one or more fields. BIRT sees what you are trying to do and un-merges the merged column, then applies the group.

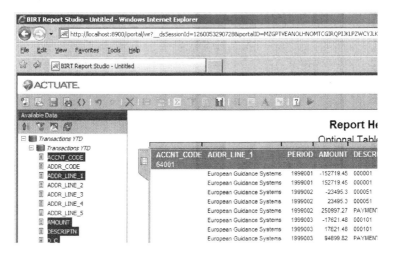

It is possible of course to select grouping of multiple fields, one after another in a nested approach, however in our example we want to keep the account code and description together in a single merged and grouped column and another approach to this is to use computed columns.

COMPUTED COLUMNS

Computed columns allow us to create new columns on our report that were not there before, so long as they are based on existing columns available in the data set. This means that we can create a computed column containing both our account code and our customer name and then group on that new single column.

To insert a new computed column click on the column of the report adjacent to where you want the computed column to appear. Then click the calculator button at the top of the designer and select New Computed Column.

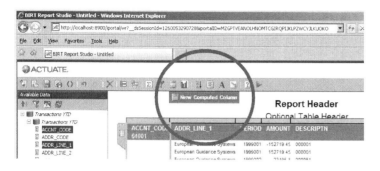

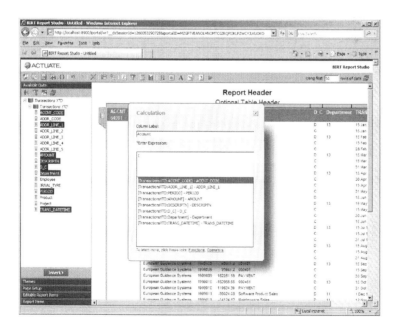

Use the pop up dialogue to name your column then start typing in the Expression box. If you enter an open square bracket "[" the system will automatically prompt you with a list of available fields. In our case we are going to select the account code field, then type in an ampersand character "&" followed by the ADDR_Line_1 field.

This will give us an expression like this:

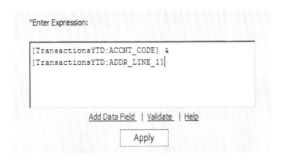

Another way of selecting fields is to click the Add Data Field link, which will present you with a dialogue containing a list of fields with check boxes. You can check the fields you wish to add and click the Apply button.

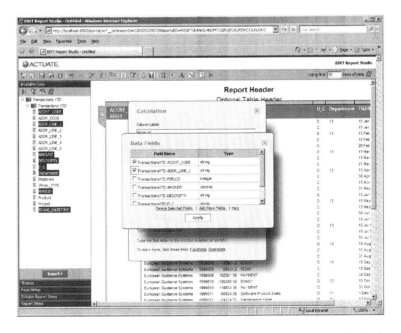

Learn more about the available functions and operators using the help system, available by clicking the links at the bottom of the Calculation dialogue. When the help system opens it is useful to click the button at the top left to open the contents page. Note that computed columns are not available to new reports that you create from the same data set. If you find that you are using a computed column regularly then it would be a good idea to ask your IT department to add it as part of the data set.

STRING FUNCTIONS

While we are here, there are a couple of other things we need to do to our report using computed columns. Our period field contains an accounting period in the form 1999001 where 1999 is the year and 001 is the month. Ideally we would like to present this to the user as 01/1999. This is where I had to get a little creative to overcome some limitations of my source data and a small limitation in BIRT itself.

Initially I thought that I could simply format the period value using a format such as @@@@/@@@ to return 1999/004 – admittedly not quite the desired result but I would have settled for that as a quick fix. Unfortunately my database value was an integer, so could not be formatted by a string function.

Still not a problem, I could go back to the data source and modify it to output the period value as a string. I modified the SQL query and used the cast statement to achieve this. Then returning to my report I found that BIRT was displaying my newly stringed field as 1,999,004 (with the commas!). OK still not too much of a problem, all I would need to do is use a left function to isolate the month, a right function to isolate the first character of the year and a mid function to isolate the last three characters of the year.

That is when I discovered that there is no mid function available within BIRT Report Studio. I could have overcome this by using a combination of the left and right functions as follows:

RIGHT(LEFT([fieldname],(LEN([fieldname])-4)),(LEN([fieldname])-5))

Ultimately I solved the problem by going back to the data designer once again and performing the string manipulation at the SQL query level. By switching into SQL mode in the report designer I would not be able to access the visual data source tools for this Information Object any more, but it goes to show that SQL level strign manipulation can be a useful tool.

This demonstrates that the BIRT applications can generally be used to solve most problems but that you do have to get creative sometimes. Hopefully in future editions functions like mid will become available.

MATHEMATICAL FUNCTIONS

Next I need to switch the signs on my value column. The system I am reporting against shows debit values, against customer accounts with a minus sign. This is fairly typical but when showing sales values on a report it is best to show them as positive values. I decided to use a mathematical function to multiply the value column by -1 to turn all negative numbers into positive and vice versa. Here is the function I used:

[TransactionsYTD:AMOUNT]*-1

The result was one column with all the negative numbers and my new computed column with them all shown as positive numbers.

Period	AMOUNT	Value	DESCRIPTN
04/1999	-217331.53	217331.53	000151
06/1999	-199710.05	199710.05	000251
10/1999	-182088.58	182088.58	000451
07/1999	-164467.1	164467.1	000301
01/1999	-152719.45	152719.45	000001
09/1999	-93981.2	93981.2	000401
12/1999	-90412.02	90412.02	Software Product Sales
08/1999	-82233.55	82233.55	000351
11/1999	-80024.08	80024.08	Software Product Sales
06/2000	-27596.52	27596.52	Multi-Currency: Goods & Servic
06/2000	-26854.98	26854.98	Multi-Currency: Goods & Servic
02/1999	-23495.3	23495.3	000051
06/1999	-23495.3	23495.3	000201
07/2000	-20697.39	20697.39	Sales (from Inventory) and Ser
12/1999	-18082.4	18082.4	Maintenance Sales
03/1999	-17621.48	17621.48	000101
07/2000	-17419.14	17419.14	Sales (from Inventory) and Ser
07/2000	15242.22	15242.22	Sales (from Inventory) and Ser

I deleted the original amount column, formatted the new value column as currency and achieved the result I needed.

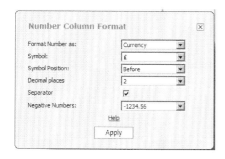

Period	Value	DESCRIPTN
04/1999	£217,331.53	000151
06/1999	£199,710.05	000251
10/1999	£182,088.58	000451
07/1999	£164,467.10	000301
01/1999	£152,719.45	000001
09/1999	£93,981.20	000401
12/1999	£90,412.02	Software Product Sales
08/1999	£82,233.55	000351
11/1999	£80,024.08	Software Product Sales
06/2000	£27,596.52	Multi-Currency: Goods & Services SO Entry
06/2000	£26,854.98	Multi-Currency: Goods & Services SO Entry
02/1999	£23,495.30	000051
06/1999	£23,495.30	000201
07/2000	£20,697.39	Sales (from Inventory) and Service
12/1999	£18,082.40	Maintenance Sales
03/1999	£17,621.48	000101
07/2000	£17,419.14	Sales (from Inventory) and Service

DELETING COLUMNS

When you create computed columns that are based on other columns, the original columns are still left on your report. Obviously you need to delete these to leave just the computed columns visible. Even though you have based a computed column on other columns, when you delete those other columns the computed columns still function correctly.

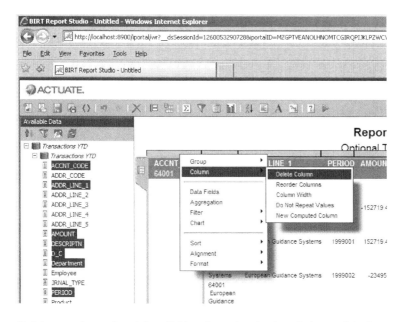

Delete a column by right clicking it and selecting Column / Delete Column.

RESIZING COLUMNS

Our new Account column is a little narrow for the data it contains, so to resize it we right click the column and select Column / Column Width, then enter a new width for the column.

Next I applied grouping to the Account and Period columns and achieved the following result.

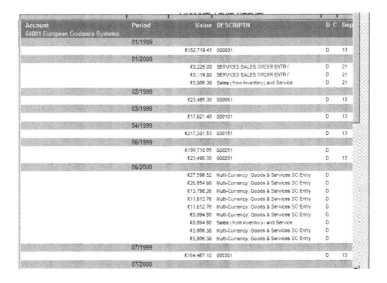

We can see that the transactions are grouped by a nicely formatted period within a nicely formatted Account code and customer name.

SUBTOTALS

Since I am grouping my report by period and account I want to add subtotals by those same levels. Doing this is simply a matter of selecting and right clicking the column you wish to add a sum to and selecting *Aggregation*.

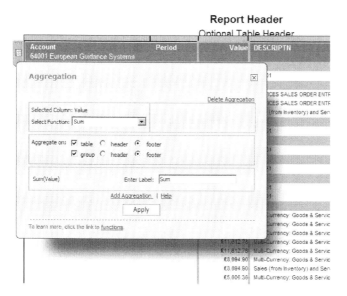

The Aggregation dialogue allows you to select what type of aggregation you need (in my case a simple sum) and where it will appear. For my example I only need to sum the individual accounts and periods, but not the entire table, so I uncheck the table option.

The result is my report now has a footer under each period and each account section containing the appropriate sum.

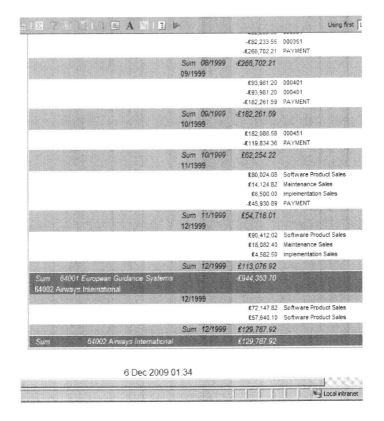

6 Dec 2009 01:34

CHARTS

Every good report needs a chart and BIRT makes adding charts very straightforward. Simply click on the chart button in the toolbar and you are presented with a dialogue asking what type of chart you want.

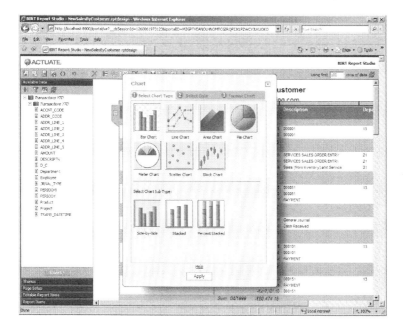

Next you select the second tab in which you can select the data for your chart, from the fields on your report. Even the calculated columns are available.

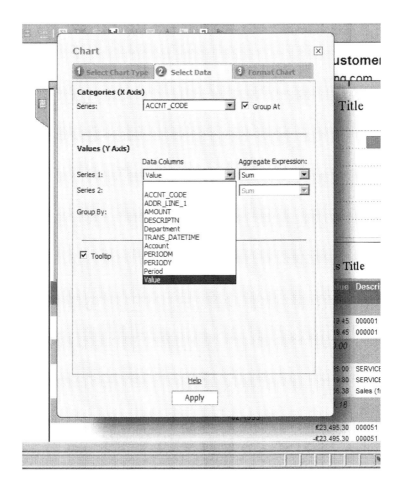

Finally you format the chart using the third tab.

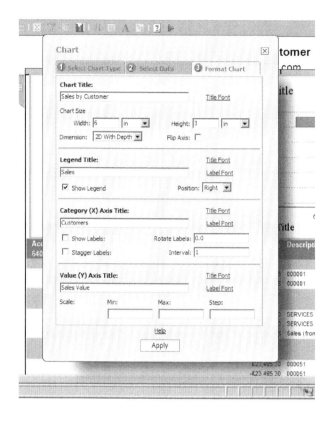

The final report including the chart looks like this

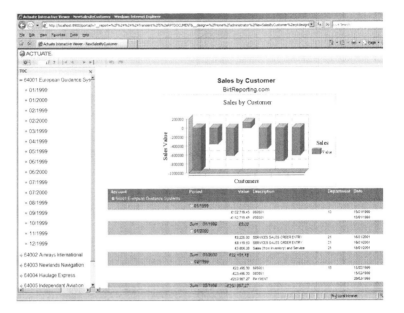

Notice that I have enabled interactivity in the BIRT Report Viewer allowing me to provide a menu based on the grouping levels and other useful functionality. To find out more about this please see the earlier section on the Interactive Viewer and iServer Express.

FILTERING AND PARAMETERS

One final point, is that large reports can often leave charts looking overcrowded. In order to present a manageable volume of data it is worth adding some filter criteria so that the report can be generated on a sub set of the full data set. To add simple filters, select the column you wish to filter on and click the filter button in the toolbar.

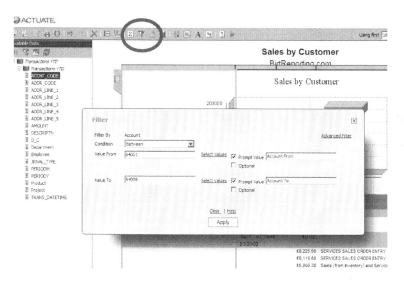

The filter dialogue allows you to predefine value ranges for your selected column and the Prompt Value fields allow these filters to become user modifiable parameters at run time.

Once I had added account code ranges to my report I was able to click the parameters option in the Interactive Viewer and adjust the report parameters whilst viewing the report.

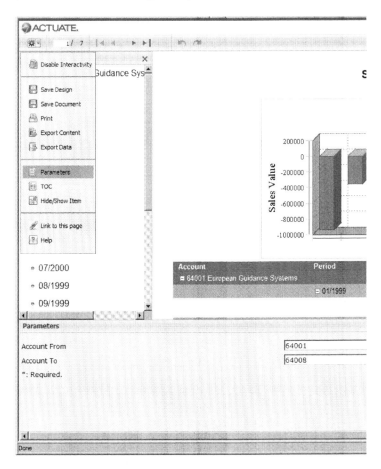

SAVING THE REPORT

Click the save button on the toolbar and you will be presented with your iServer Express directory structure. Select a folder and name your report. Once saved it will become available from the folder structure on the iServer Express main screen. From there you will be able to run and modify your report, with all the report interactivity that the Interactive Viewer provides.

SUMMARY WEB BASED REPORT DESIGN

The BIRT Repot Studio really does make it possible for the end user to create, save, run and modify their own reports entirely over the web, with no software to install on the client side. It stops short of being an advanced report writer, with certain small limitations, but since it is a tool designed for the end user this should not be a problem.

IT resources still need to provide the basic underlying data that end user reports will be based on. This does need to be provided intelligently, in line with the users reporting requirements and will mean that communication between line of business end users and IT resources will need to take place to plan the data requirements.

I imagine that this will take the form of a consultative approach on the part of the IT resources who are the keepers of the data and an educational one on the part of the business users, who understand the data and what it represents.

SECTION 7

FORMATTING BIRT REPORTS

Here we look at some of the formatting possibilities to get you started making your reports presentable for the public. These techniques work equally well in the open source and commercial versions.

ABOUT REPORT FORMATTING

When creating reports it is important to spend some time thinking about the format of the report so that it is easy on the eye, looks professional and groups of data, with headers, content and footers are easily distinguishable.

In this section we look at some basic data formatting options.

We are going to base this on a simple customer listing, which features the name and address of the customer in a group, with telephone and fax numbers on the first line of the group. The address is contained in the first column of the report. Here is our basic, unformatted report layout.

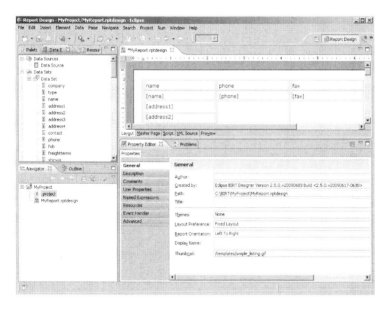

BACKGROUND AND FOREGROUND

To start with we are going to give the column headings some prominence with a black background and white text.

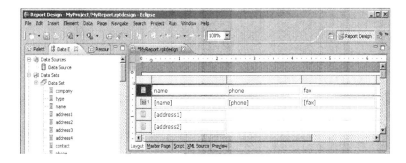

Start by selecting the header row by clicking first on the table tab and then on the cell to the very left of the row.

Now select the Property Editor tab in the bottom pane of the screen. Ensure that Properties and General are selected.

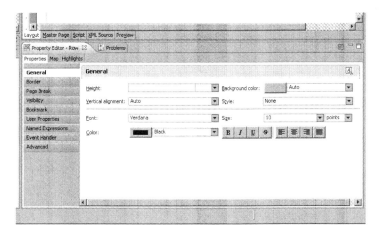

Here we can see several formatting options which will be applied to the currently selected row. It is possible to select the height, vertical alignment, font, font size, background and foreground colours and effects such as bold and italics.

For our example we are going to make the background black, the foreground white and the font bold. We use the same tools to set the properties of the group header, this time we select a light grey background, leave the font black and not bold.

Our report design looks like this:

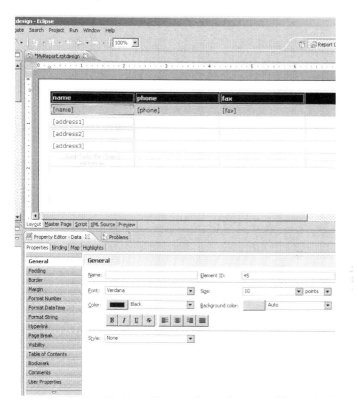

And our previewed report looks like this:

name	phone	fax
AMM Intenational P.O. Box 1335, 1200 BH Hilversum The Netherlands Tel.:+31 35 6881211	+31 35 6881211	+31 35 6834161
Avis Rent a Car 1st Flr. 1 Station Rd, Pangbourne, Reading, RG8 7AN, UK Tel.:+44 118 9841040	+44 118 9841040	+44 118 9845060
BARTEC Gmbh Max-Eyth-Str. 16, PO Box 1166 D-97980 Bad Mergentheim Germany	+49 (0) 7931 597-0	+49 (0) 7931 597-119
Baker Industrial Supplies St. Martin House, 77 Wales St., Winchester, Hamshire, SO23 ORH England	+44 1962 860331	+44 1962 841339
British Airways P.O. Box 1220 D-74668 Forchtenberg Germany	+49 7947 828619	+49 7947 828619
British Midland Schurwaldstr. 9 73765 Neuhausen a.d.F., Germany Tel.:+49 7158 173 136	+49 7158 173 136	+49 7158 173 286
British Telecom Gydevang 32-34 3450 Allerod - Denmark Tel.:+45 48168072	+45 48168072	+45 48168080
Browns Bar and Braserie	+49 2039923-160	+49 203 259 1

PADDING AND BORDERS

Now we are going to add another two design aspects to differentiate the groups from each other.

Firstly we are going to add some padding to the last cell of the group, so that some space appears between the last address row and the first row of the next record.

To do this we select the cell that we wish to pad, then in the Padding property, increase the bottom padding value to 10 points.

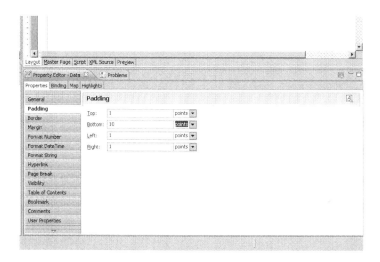

Next we are going to add a top and bottom border to the name / phone / fax line

To do this we select the three cells, by using the shift key whilst clicking on the cells we require. Then we select the Border property and click on the two left most buttons, which apply top and bottom borders. The other buttons can be used to apply left/right and all round borders.

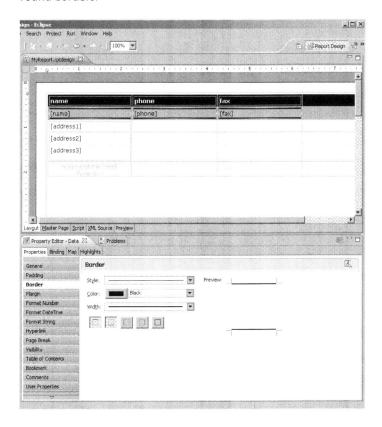

Now our report looks like this:

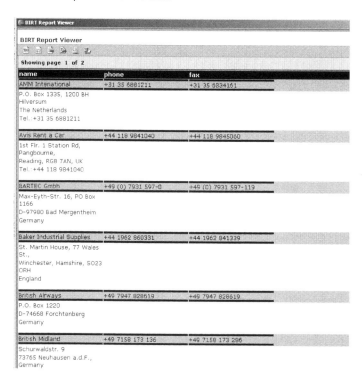

You may have noticed by now that not all the properties are available to all areas of the report. For example unless you have selected a cell or group of cells the border property is not visible.

MARGINS

The same applies to the margin property, this can be used to set margins for specific cells, groups of cells or the entire table. By selecting the table and increasing the margin to 10 all round, we add a little whitespace between the report viewer edges and the actual data.

And the effect on the report is like this:

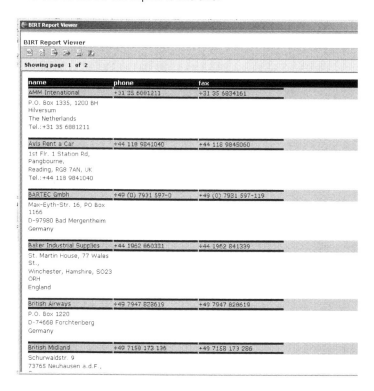

We have seen how to manually add different formatting options to various sections of our report. BIRT however allows us to use styles, which means that we can define the properties of our style and then apply it easily to other sections of the report simply by selecting the style rather than having to manually format each area.

To define a style select a cell, in our case the "Name" header cell, right click it and select *Style / New Style*

The Style dialogue appears:

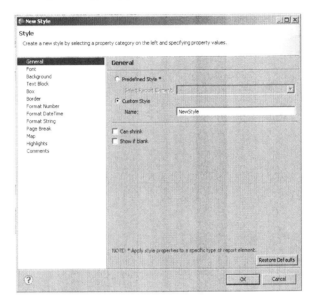

We replace the default name "New Style" with our own name, e.g. Header then modify the font, background and border properties as appropriate. When we have finished we click OK and we can see our new style is applied to our selected cell. Now we can select the other cells of the header row, right click them and select *Style / Apply Style / Header* and our header style is applied to the selected cells.

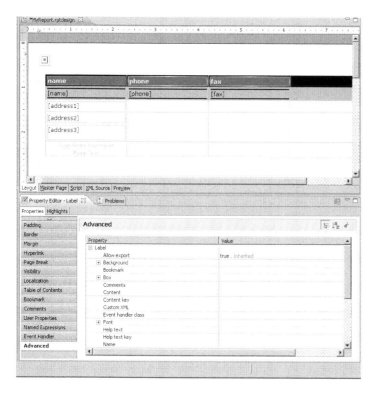

Of course a style can be edited, simply right click the styled cell(s) and select Style / Edit Style

Certain style items can be applied to the entire report, for example you may wish to fix the font in order to override any local browser settings that may exist in the viewers browser. To do this open the styles node of the outline explorer and locate the report style. Double click it and select a font that is different to your standard report font. Then click OK. You will see that the entire report font is changed.

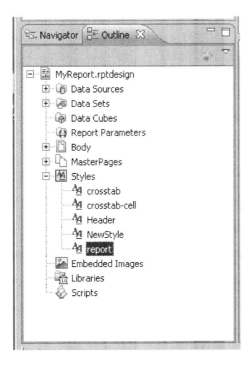

REPORT HEADINGS

The Grid control can be used to define headings for the report. To apply a grid, drag the grid control from the palette to the area above your report layout. The grid dialogue is displayed.

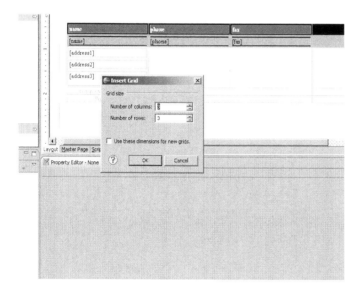

Accept the defaults and a grid is displayed in your report design.

We can set each column of the grid to be exactly 33% of the width of the report so that the heading fills the entire width and we can set the alignment of the first column to left, the middle column to middle and the right column to right, so that the headings we place in the cells look nicely aligned.

To do this select the column header of each column of the grid and apply the justification and width settings as appropriate. To set the width to 33%, simply enter 33 into the width field and select % from the drop down menu.

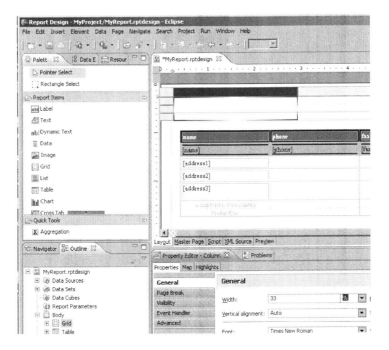

Now we can add an image to our report. Drag the image object from the palette into the first cell of the grid.

The image dialogue is displayed. From here you can browse to the image file you want to insert.

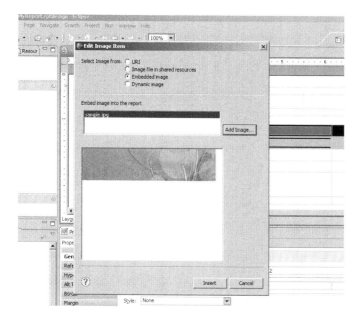

Next drag the label object to the centre of the grid and add some text.

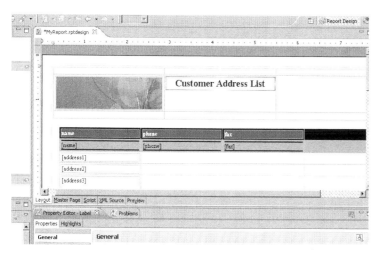

Then finally drag a data object to the last cell and insert the current date by completing the dialogue as below.

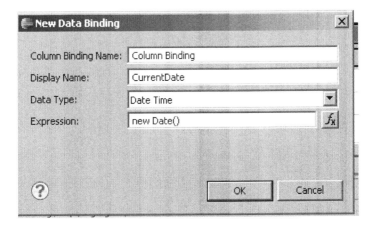

Running the report shows that our header image, title and current date are applied as expected.

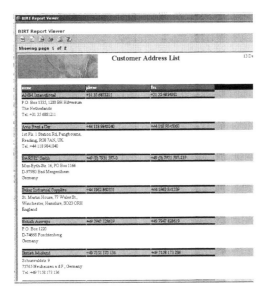

ALTERNATE ROW COLOURS

A nice touch to reports that list records is to alternate the background colour of every other row. This can be achieved by selecting the detail row of the report and clicking on the highlights tab in the lower pane. Then clicking the add button to create a new highlight.

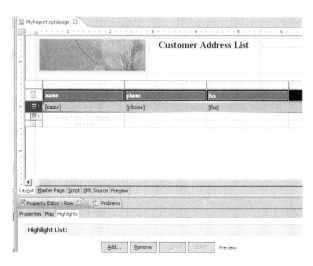

In the dialogue enter the condition

Row["__Rownum"]%2

That is a double underscore in front of Rownum by the way.

Then select the Equal to operator and type 0 into the final field. Now select the colour for your alternating rows, click OK and preview the report.

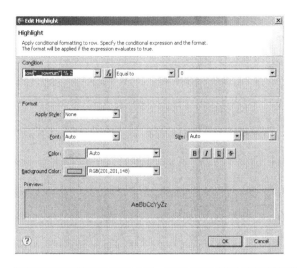

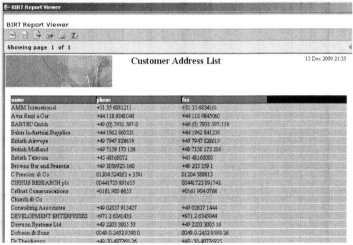

Feel free to play around with the various formatting options and see what you can achieve.

There are additional tips and tricks always being added to the archive at BIRTReporting.com which will help with more advanced formatting options.

SECTION 8

BIRT SPREADSHEET DESIGNER

The BIRT Spreadsheet Designer is a free tool from Actuate that allows you to create data driven spreadsheet reports that can simultaneously access data from multiple different databases and be deployed over the web using iServer Express.

ABOUT BIRT SPREADSHEET

First a little about the name of this product. BIRT Spreadsheet started it's life as something called e.Spreadsheet Designer and was a free product from Actuate, as opposed to an open source product built on the Eclipse platform. After the success of the open source strategy with BIRT it appears that Actuate have decided to rebrand e.Spreadsheet Designer as BIRT Spreadsheet. The rebranding is currently fairly superficial because at many points in the software and in the help system the software is still referred to as e.Spreadsheet Designer – take a look at the installer sceenshot below.

Don't let this put you off though, because even if the look and feel is slightly different from the way BIRT operates, this is still a strong, useful and genuinely free product that you can use to create data driven spreadsheets, that is spreadsheets that can pull data dynamically from any ODBC compliant data source, that end users can get to grips with quickly and intuitively because it is based on traditional spreadsheet design concepts which many users will already be familiar with.

You need to invest in the iServer Express so that your spreadsheet designs can be deployed within the iServer directory structure, alongside your other BIRT reports and accessed by users over the web, alternatively you could deploy the designer software to each workstation where BIRT Spreadsheets need to be used.

I look forward to seeing how this product develops over the coming months but for now here is my introductory quick start guide that should have you up and running and experiencing what BIRT Spreadsheets has to offer.

WHAT TO DOWNLOAD

Here is the download location – the file size is 339Mb and you need to be a member of BIRT-Exchange to gain access, but BE is free to join and the tool is free to use.

http://www.BIRT-exchange.org/downloads/spreadsheet-automation/239-BIRT-spreadsheet-designer-for-windows-release-10-sp1/

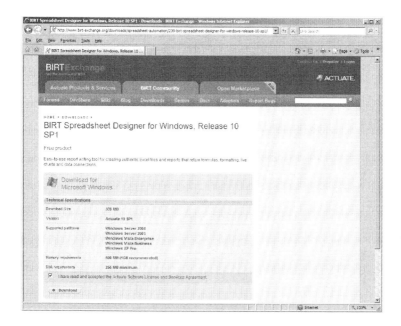

INSTALLATION

Installation is simplicity itself, just run the download package and follow the installation wizard, accepting all the defaults. Be aware that the installation requires a restart of the PC – I'm not sure if this is required on all operating systems, but I installed on Windows XP Professional so assume a restart will be required to be on the safe side and don't install it on a production server in the middle of the day!

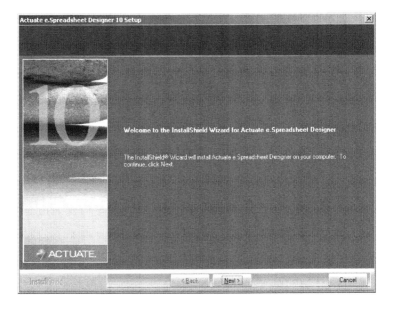

CREATING A DATA SOURCE

In order to create a BIRT spreadsheet report the first thing you need to do is create a data source. This is fairly similar to how data sources are created in BIRT but not exactly the same.

Start by launching the application, by default the installer does not place an icon on your desktop so you can find it by going to Start / Programs / Actuate 10 / e.Spreadsheet Designer.

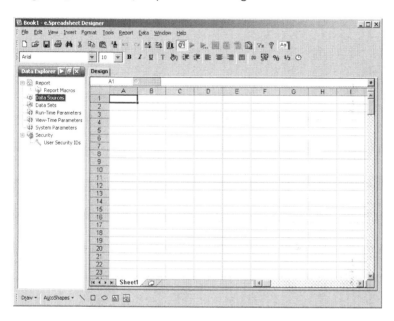

The designer window opens with a spreadsheet view and a data explorer tree on the left hand side. Right click on Data Sources and select Create Data Source. This will launch the Data Source wizard.

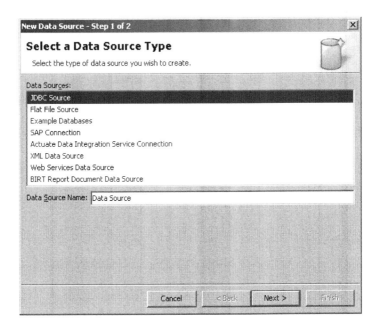

There are a number of data source types available, including flat file, XML, Web services and BIRT Reports – so you can actually use a BIRT report to build a spreadsheet from! For my example I am going to select JDBC source and point it at my SQL Server.

Next comes a standard data source form which should be completed as in the screenshot below. Once done you can test the data source to see if it is working.

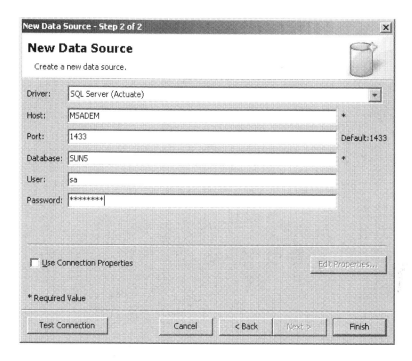

Once your data source is created you need to create a data set, this is achieved by right clicking on the Data Source which has now appeared in the tree on the left and selecting Create Data Set.

The defaults are fine to use for a simple query but note that you can also use stored procedure calls here, which is useful if you use the same data sets in many different reports.

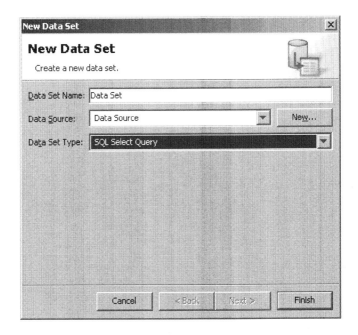

On finishing the creation, the list of tables from your selected database is displayed. You can click on multiple tables and add them to the designer, using the add button.

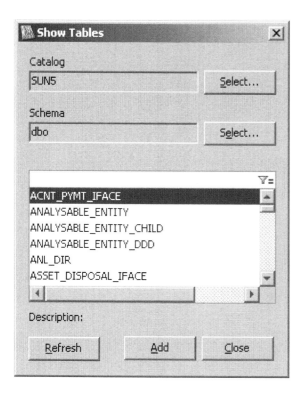

Many databases are complex and have a long list of tables. The white space immediately above the table list is in fact a search box. If you start typing the name of the table you want the list is immediately filtered.

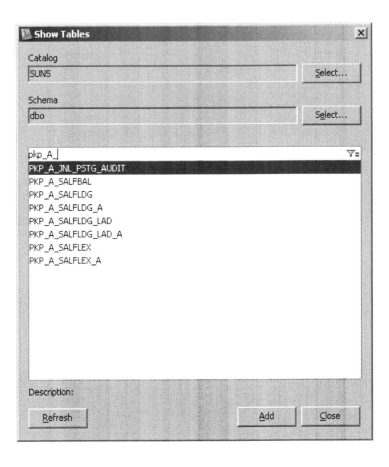

Once you have added some tables they can be linked by dragging the related field from one table to the related field on the other.

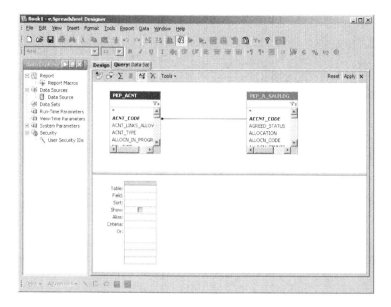

Next you can drag the fields you require in your data set into the grid below. You have to be careful to drag the fields to just over the grey table header before you are allowed to drop them. Once dropped the field appears in the table and a new column appears ready to accept the next field. You can enter alias field names here and filter criteria if you need to present only a subset of your data.

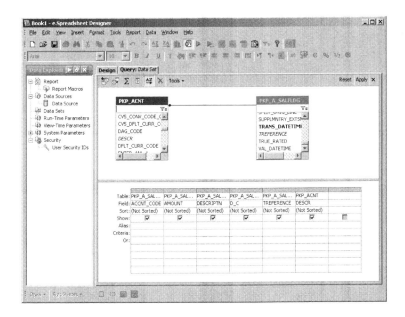

Click Apply and your data set is added to the tree.

CREATE QUICK REPORT

It is easy to create a quick listing of data using the Listing Wizard. Switch to Design mode, by clicking on the Design tab, then select Report / Listing Wizard and from the dialogue that appears select the data set that you wish to use.

If you wish you can apply some sorting and grouping at the next screen.

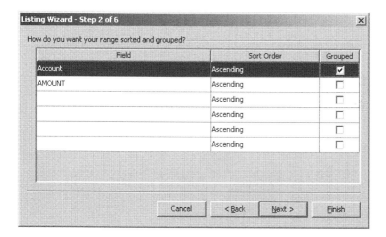

Next you can select the field that you wish to display in the output.

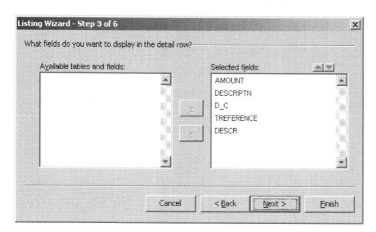

Next you apply the sums that are required.

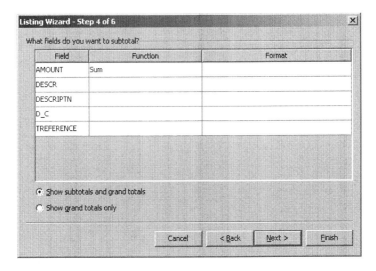

Finally you select the format and style of the report and hit finish.

RUNNING YOUR REPORT

BIRT Spreadsheet reports are executed in the designer by clicking the green "play" button on the toolbar.

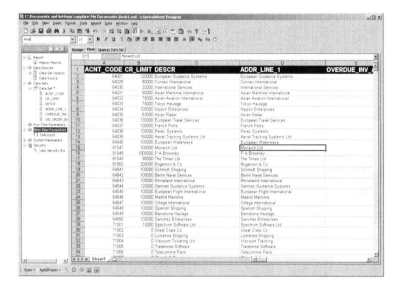

The report is displayed in the spreadsheet window.

ADDING PARAMETERS

It is possible to add runtime parameters to your report so that the end user can select the data range on which to report. To do this, right click on the Run-Time Parameters item in the data explorer and select *Create Report Parameter*. The parameter configuration dialogue is displayed.

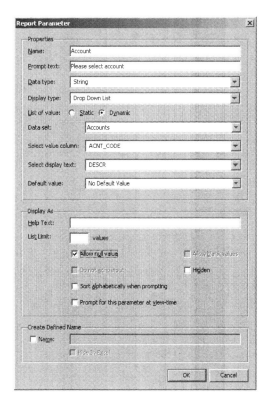

First name your parameter, in my case I intend to allow the user to select which account code the report will show. Next enter the text that you wish displayed to the user at runtime. Then select the data type of the field that will be accepting the data – this should be the same as the database field against which it will be compared. In my case the account code field on my database is a string field, so I make my parameter a string field too.

Next you can select the type of entry that the user is to perform when entering the parameter.

The options are:

- Text Box – which simply allows the user to type in a value

- Drop Down List – which allows the user to select a single choice from a number of options in a list

- Combo Box – which allows the user to select multiple items from a list

- Radio Button – which allows the user to select a single item from a number of items displayed as "buttons"

I am going to use the Drop Down List for my example. Once selected you can either type in the values that you want the user to select from, or, you can populate the list dynamically from a table in the database. This is great because if, as in my case, you want the user to select from a range of data that will be constantly evolving, this ensures that the latest values are always available.

Note, that dynamic drop downs can't be based on the main query of the report, so you will need to create a separate data set from which to select the dynamic data. Once you have done this, simply select the new data set and the column that will be selected. You can also select the display column – so in my example I want the account code to be selected but I want the user to see the account name.

To make the report filter by the parameter value, return to the data set query and enter the parameter name with a colon at the beginning into the criteria field for the column that you with to filter by.

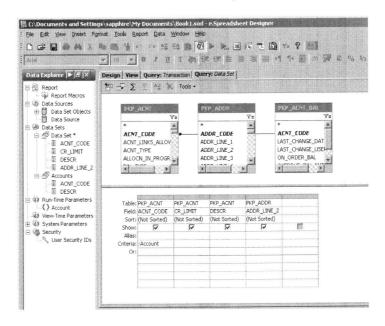

In my example I am allowing the user to select an account code, so I place the filter into the account code column.

To run your report and invoke the parameter, press the green "play" arrow with the three dots under it.

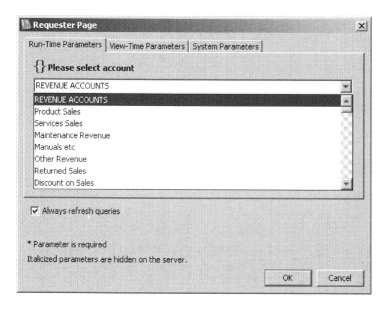

This time the first thing that appears is the parameter selection box.

CUSTOM REPORTS

So far we have used the listing wizard to create a straightforward listing for us, but what if we want to get a bit more adventurous and create a master / detail report. For our example I am going to create a report that shows account details such as account number, account name and credit limit at the top and a list of transactions below that, the user will be able to select the account code to list.

To start with I create 2 data sets as before, one with the account header information and one with a simple listing of accounts, to be used for the parameter selection. Then I add a further data set, which is a listing of transactions, importantly this has a common account code field with the accounts listing, so I am able to filter my transaction data set by exactly the same parameter I filtered the accounts listing by. This means that when the report runs, both the accounts data set and the transactions data set are filtered on the same account code value, thus showing me a single account and a listing of transactions for that account.

Next we need to create a data range – this is an area on the spreadsheet where the report data will go. It was created automatically by the report wizard, but because we are not using the wizard this time we need to create it manually.

Do this by selecting the design view, then the Report menu and finally click on Create Data Range.

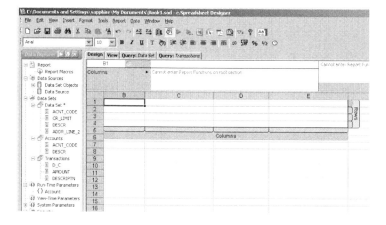

You will see that a section with rows and columns is created.

Now you can start to insert your header fields, by simply dragging them from the data set on the left and dropping them where you want them to appear. When you drop a field the insert report function dialogue appears, in this case we want to select the Write command, the Accounts data set and the field name corresponding to the field we are dropping. Usually these selections are made for you by default.

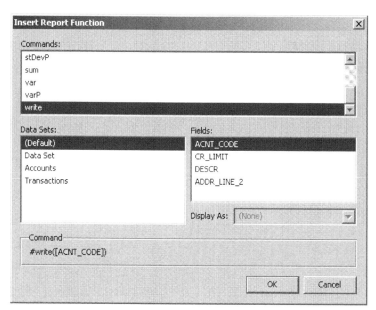

After inserting all my fields into the first three rows of the report, I use some standard spreadsheet cell formatting commands to add a little design to the report.

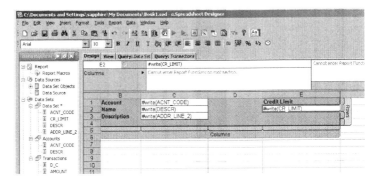

Now we need to insert the detail lines from the transactions data set. To do this we need to add a little space between our header and lines section and enable the detail section of the report to hold repeating data. Right click on the mini tab to the right of the last row and select Insert Row Before – this provides our spacer row.

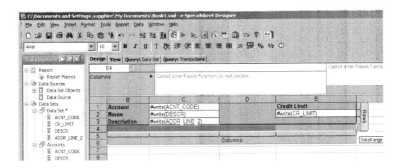

Next right click on the mini tab on the last row again and select Create Parent – then name the section in the dialogue that appears. The named section will be displayed in the report layout.

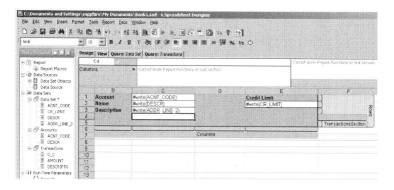

Next, right click the new section tab and select Group. In the group dialogue check the "output data rows" check box and select the detail data set to use. In my case I want to use the transactions data set I created earlier.

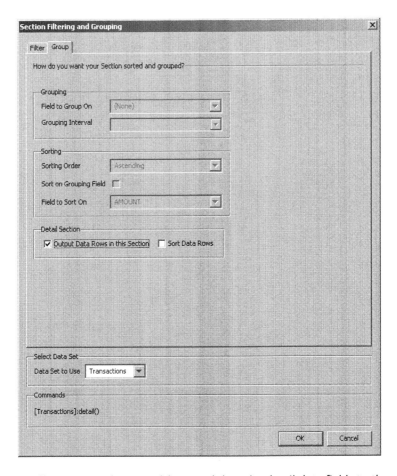

Finally return to the spreadsheet and drag the detail data fields to the new section, add a bit of formatting and you are done.

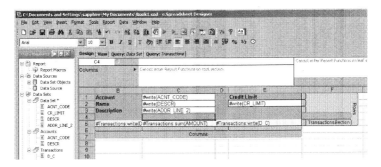

Now when we run the report and include parameters we can select the account code and are presented with a listing of transactions for the selected account.

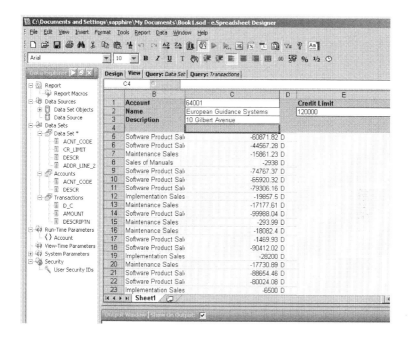

OUTPUT AS EXCEL OR PDF

It is also possible to output your report as an Excel spreadsheet or a PDF file, simply by pressing the Excel or PDF buttons on the toolbar.

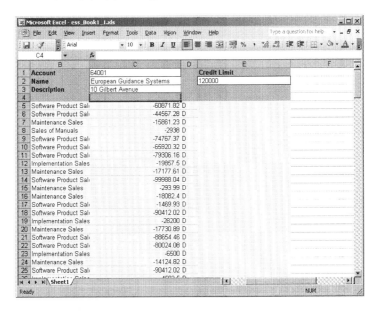

The report in Excel

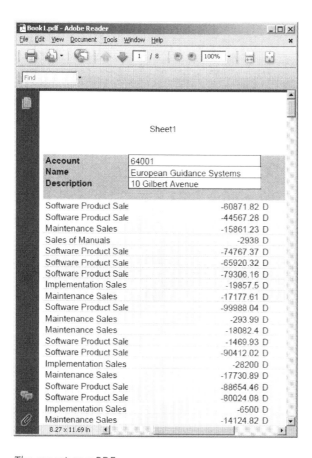

The report as a PDF

SUMMARY OF BIRT SPREADSHEET DESIGNER

In this section we have looked at how to create data driven spreadsheets with the BIRT Spreadsheet Designer.

This has been a quick overview of some of the main features but there are plenty more to explore which will allow you to easily create attractive and useful spreadsheet based reports which can be deployed over the web and scheduled, using Actuate's iServer Express.

I would encourage you to learn more about the power of this product by using the help system which provides detailed instructions on the more advanced features. Also keep an eye on BIRTReporting.com for detailed guides and training options.

SECTION 9

CONCLUSION

RETURN ON INVESTMENT

Whilst reviewing the commercial add-ons to BIRT I am constantly thinking about the additional value that these tools may or may not provide to the business community. When it is possible to do all of your reporting, over the web, using the freely available open source tools, then added value must be a consideration when thinking about spending money on additional commercial aspects of this software.

In thinking about this I have considered the work that an IT resource would have to undertake in agreeing the specification of reports with the business, writing the reports, maintaining the reports and making tweaks and adjustments as the business requires. When comparing this to the simple production of data sets, on which end users could write their own reports it is easy to see that the business case for the additional cost of iServer Express and the BIRT Report Studio depends very much on two key factors.

1. The time spent by specialised and expensive IT resources in meeting user reporting demands.

2. The time users have to wait to get the reports they need.

Clearly the direct salary cost is not the only factor because the provision of the right information at the right time can be as far reaching as gaining a business a competitive edge or being able to give customers the information they need when they need it.

Every business is different and has different reporting needs and time scales. The BIRT stable of tools fits into practically any business because you can start off with a no cost simple solution and scale it incrementally as the business requirement dictates.

In creating this book I have looked closely at how IT resources would create and publish data to their end user community and allow those users to write reports based on that data. Once again I find that

Actuate have put a lot of thought into the user experience and the Information Object designer is logical and easy to use. Conceptually it breaks down the task of creating reports into distinct data and application layers and provides easy delimitation between the users of each part.

If your business demands warrant it then these tools provide an exceptional way to hand over business report generation to your user community.

AUTHORS NOTE

I hope you have enjoyed reading this as much as I have enjoyed writing it and that it has proved to be a useful introduction to the BIRT report writing tools.

The primary aim of this book is to quickly provide you with enough information about BIRT so that you can make an informed decision about including it in the portfolio of products that are used within your organisation. Or if you are an independent consultant to help you decide if you wish to learn more about BIRT so that you can offer related services to your clients.

If you have been following the tutorials in this book then you will already know a lot about the product suite and have a good understanding of how to create and deploy reports and which tools to use for the job.

All in all I believe that BIRT is a well thought out, easy to use product that can help you easily generate good looking reports fast and accurately. It is also a product with a good future because unlike many open source products it has a commercial angle to it and is backed by one of the world's foremost reporting software companies.

I am looking forward to seeing how BIRT develops over the coming years, how many companies deploy it as the standard report writer in their own products and how the worldwide community of BIRT experts continues to grow.

Most of all though I am looking forward to bringing you more information on this product on the BIRTReporting.com web site and hopefully meeting some of you at the regular BIRT User Group UK meetings.

FURTHER READING

Please visit http://www.BIRTReporting.com where you will be able to find lots of goodies to download.

Look for the "BIRT for Beginners" section of the web site where, as an owner of this book, you will be able to log in to a special "readers only" area.

Here you will find additional chapters which you can use as companion reading material and forms that you can use to give to your end users which they can complete to request reports and Information Objects from you.

If you would like to gain a deeper understanding of BIRT then I recommend the following books and web sites. All this and more is available from ...

http://www.BIRTReporting.com

INFORMATION OBJECT FORM

Download the original PDF version of this form from http://www.BIRTReporting.com and use it within your organisation to simplify the process of request and specification of BIRT Information Objects.

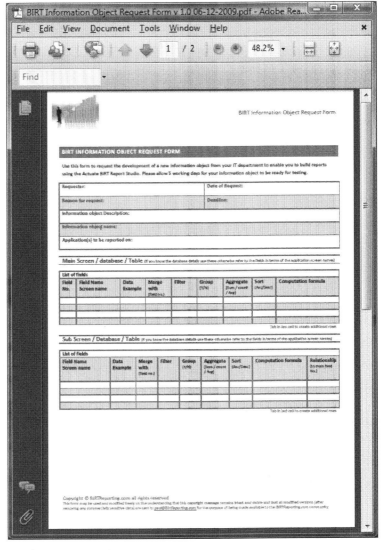

REPORT REQUEST FORM

Similar to the Information Object request form this one simplifies the request and specification of BIRT reports. Download the PDF from http://www.BIRTReporting.com

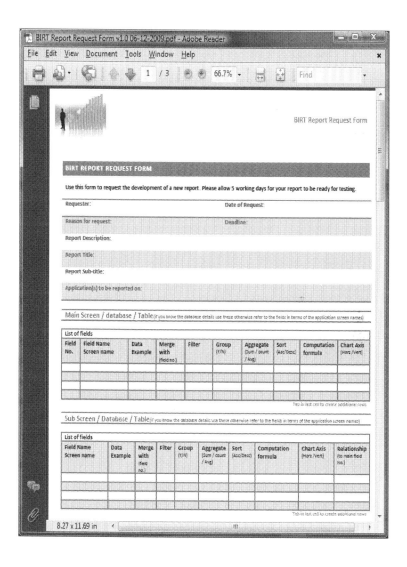

BOOKS

Gain a deep understanding of BIRT with these excellent books.

BIRT A Field Guide to Reporting

Integrating and Extending BIRT

The Definitive Guide to Eclipse BIRT

Practical Data Analysis and Reporting with BIRT

Buy these online at:

http://www.BIRTReporting.com/Books-on-BIRT-Reports.html

WEB SITES

There is plenty of information available online, start with these sites.

BIRT Reporting.com

http://www.BIRTReporting.com

The Eclipse BIRT home page

http://www.eclipse.org/BIRT/

The Actuate BIRT home page

http://www.actuate.com/products/BIRT/

BIRT-Exchange

http://www.BIRT-exchange.org

BIRT World

http://BIRTworld.blogspot.com/

INDEX

31572779R00154

Made in the USA
Middletown, DE
04 May 2016